PRELIM

(A)

Title: Typing ... .
Author: John Westwood
39 Parker Street, London WC2B 5PB

THIS IS PACKET 1 OF TYPESCRIPT
See Inventory below.

22 August 1975

INVENTORY of entire typescript,
of which this packet is part:

Packet 1:
Prelims (folios A to G) and
Chapters 1 to 3 (folios 1 to 36)
Packet 2:
Chapters 4 to 6 (folios 37 to 62)
Packet 3:
Rough sketches for Figs. 1 & 2 and
copy for Tables 1 to 3
(folios 63 to 68)

HALF TITLE

PRELIM B

Typing for print

John Westwood

TITLE PAGE

PRELIM ©

Typing for print

A manual for typists and authors

John Westwood

Pitman Publishing

PRELIM

D

First published 1976

This manual is intended primarily for typists and authors. It will also be useful to designers, and to staff in printing and publishing houses. It has two aims: first, to help those wishing to learn the typing style most suited to conversion to printed form; and secondly, to provide an actual example of the recommended style. Therefore, this manual is presented as an exact facsimile of an author's typescript, although for economic reasons it has been scaled down in size. Actual typescripts should of course be executed on one side of the paper only.

PITMAN PUBLISHING LTD
Pitman House, 39 Parker Street, Kingsway, London WC2B 5PB
PO Box 46038, Banda Street, Nairobi, Kenya

PITMAN PUBLISHING PTY LTD
Pitman House, 158 Bouverie Street, Carlton, Victoria 3053
Australia

PITMAN PUBLISHING CORPORATION
6 East 43 Street, New York, NY 10017, USA

SIR ISAAC PITMAN (CANADA) LTD
495 Wellington Street West, Toronto M5V IG1, Canada

THE COPP CLARK PUBLISHING COMPANY
517 Wellington Street West, Toronto M5V IG1, Canada

ISBN: 0 273 00183 3

Camera copy prepared by Morgan-Westley

0142/41

Reproduced and printed by photolithography and bound in Great Britain at The Pitman Press, Bath.

PRELIM E

Contents

PRELIM (F)

Note to typists. Practice exercises for typists may include copying any part of this manual. The study lists 6.1 to 6.4 have been presented in run-on style in order to save space; exercises may include re-typing these lists in columns, so that they may subsequently be used more easily for reference if required.

Please note that publishers usually prefer to receive copy which has been typed on an ordinary machine on which all the characters are the same width; with such copy it is easy for the publisher to make the necessary count of the total number of characters or words. Typing on an electric machine with variable spacing is not suitable.

Introduction

Printing is expensive; an author's typescript will be welcomed by the publisher and printer, literary merit apart, if the typing style employed permits it to be turned into print easily and economically. Good typing style may be the crucial factor making it possible to reduce the costs of production and printing to a point where publication becomes economically feasible.

This manual should assist the typist thrown into a situation where he or she has to learn the needs of printers as quickly as possible. It is also intended as a guide for authors, and others involved in printing and book production. It expounds the principles laid down in the relevant BS (British Standard), and is itself a model showing how to 'type for print' in the recommended style.

The typist trained in a secretarial college will have to be prepared to unlearn certain habits, in order to be able to provide typescript according to the rules of printing rather than those of business typing. Many special features, peculiar to books, will also require study. But if the method shown in this manual is followed carefully, the typist need not worry about the subsequent extremely complicated technical work of converting the typescript into print. The publisher will find such typescript ready for editing, and for 'casting off', i.e. calculating how many pages of print would result; his staff will then be able to insert written instructions, prescribing where special spacing or typefaces should be employed in the printing. The typescript will also be processed more quickly, easily and economically by the printer.

Chapters 1 and 2 of this manual are essential reading for all purposes; the remainder is for reference as required.

1 Organizing the work

1.1 The author and the typist

Many authors type their own work. Others may engage a typist, who will share the responsibility for details in typescript, and perhaps also manage correspondence with the publisher or printer. Planning starts long before the final typescript is prepared. The author should at an early stage consider how to arrange his ideas under headings, without regimenting his readers: any book is difficult to read if it is cluttered with over-complicated systems of headings, subheadings, numbering of paragraphs, appendices, and footnotes.

The rough draft may be written, or very roughly typed, or recorded on tape; when ready for final typing, the author should label it 'PLEASE TYPE AS COPY FOR PRINTING'. To make it clear that the normal rules of business typing do not apply, typists may be asked to refer to this manual (or to the British Standard, BS 5261 Part 1).

Only the first few chapters should normally be typed for initial submission to the publisher, so that if any alterations to style are suggested they may later be incorporated more easily in the whole work. An individual typist is more likely than a typing pool to achieve consistent results for the whole of a lengthy work.

The typist's first duty is to scan the whole draft quickly, in order to assess how much interpretation will be needed. If the author has written some words in abbreviated form, the typist must judge whether or not to spell out in full. Or the copy may have been arranged in very short paragraphs, which might look wrong in print. Before starting to type, the typist must list such doubtful points of sense or style, and query them, in order to establish the overall

Type for print on one side of the paper only:
all your folios will be 'right-hand pages'.

pattern. Individual points may be self-evident, e.g. the ambiguous sense arising from a carelessly-omitted hyphen, as in twenty two ton lorries. But, 'here we go round the mulberry bush, the mulberry-bush, the mulberrybush . . .' Which is correct? Some queries may require reference to Collins or other books listed at 3.5.

No author is infallible. No typist is infallible; but a good typist will be willing and able to assist by correcting small errors, and will report any such changes made. There is a great deal of systematic work to do; authors who have skilled help are fortunate. Authors who type their own work but find that following this manual tends to inhibit creative writing may consider arranging for final re-typing by someone competent in BS style. Maintaining overall consistency of style is most difficult in works where several authors have each in turn contributed a chapter.

This manual is primarily addressed personally to the author and the typist. Together you may decide who can best draw in neatly in ink any foreign accents, mathematical signs, or other characters which do not appear on the typewriter keyboard.

If (for good reasons) unorthodox features of style are employed, these should be explained in a covering note to the publisher, who might otherwise want to alter them.

Do not try to decide whether the final printing should have centred or flush-left headings. Follow the style of this manual (i.e. flush left throughout; see also 2.10). You may leave it to the publisher to settle style, arrangement and size of all headings.

If you are ordering your own printing, type headings in your copy as in this manual, and then take advice from a professional graphic designer or from your printer.

A

1.2 Methods and margins

Three copies of the typescript will be required, so type a master copy with two carbons, or type the master copy and take two photocopies when all is complete. The latter method costs more.

Type in clear black, *on one side only* of upright A4 sheets of strong paper (A4 is 297 mm by 210 mm, i.e. $11\frac{3}{4}$ in. by $8\frac{1}{4}$ in.). Good quality thick bond paper, say '85 grams per square metre' substance, is required, to withstand not only erasure but also many handlings by the publisher's and printer's staff. Such paper costs about 2p (4 cents) per copy at 1975 prices for every thousand words.

Margins must be generous throughout: 40 mm ($1\frac{1}{2}$ in.) on the left, and 25 mm (1 in.) on the right and at head and foot. These margins are *not* wasteful but normal and necessary.

Double-space throughout. Start each chapter on a fresh sheet of paper. Start each text paragraph with a three-space indent. Do not put extra space between paragraphs. Type only one space after a full point, semicolon, colon, or comma.

Each sheet of typescript is called a folio; each holds about 300 words. The numbering of folios will be different from the numbering of the final *printed pages*, because the latter may each hold 400 words or more. If you wanted to refer the reader to folio 279, show thus: See also p. 000 (folio 279). The printer will set the 000 in type. The page proofs will reveal the numbers of the printed pages, and on these proofs you will alter each 000 to the proper number.

The overall aim is clarity rather than absolute neatness. Details of typing style follow in Chapter 2 onwards; but as a preview a list of the main principles now follows.

O (4)

[B] Short summary of the entire manual

Always use A4 paper, one side only. Margins: on left 1½ in., others 1 in.; type with double spacing.

Type headings flush left as in this manual; no full point: never CAPS or CAPS. Mark chapters as [Chap], and subheadings as [A], [B].

Indent paragraphs three spaces; do not put extra space between paragraphs. Never hyphenate at end of a line. Carry whole word over.

Type hyphen as in hi-fi, long-term; but check in Collins or the C.O.D. (see 3.5) whether words should be separate or hyphenated or joined up. Type unspaced double hyphen for spans, as 1914--18, the London--Dover road. Type spaced double hyphen -- as here -- for dash (pause). Type treble hyphen for omitted part thus ---. See 2.2.

Omit full point in contractions Mr Mrs Messrs Dr Revd Bt St; in abbreviations BBC IOU ITV MP (plural MPs); Unesco, NATO; short forms Pan Am, exam; metric symbols (SI) e.g. cm m km g kg (plurals same: no s). Then make your own 'omit points' list: see 2.7.

Retain full points in all other abbreviations including i.e. e.g. a.m. p.m. and names, decorations and qualifications thus: J. B. Grey, C.B.E., F.R.Hist.S. Plurals thus: N.C.O.s etc.

Single space after punctuation, as here. Italic for emphasis, and for non-naturalized foreign words, titles of books, ships, works of art: à deux, Roget's Thesaurus, H.M.S. Victory, Mona Lisa.

Spell out most non-technical numbers. See 2.9. Dates: as Thursday 13 May 1974 (no commas). Addresses: as 143 High Street, London SE1 2BN.

Standard decimal points as 0.5; or centred as 0·5. Large numbers as 1,234,567 but in technical work as 1 234 567 (thin space). Insert in ink: [] é etc.

References in text to books thus: (see Lockwood, A., Diagrams, Studio Vista, 1969). Turnover indent styles: see p. 00 (folio 34).

A

1.3 Prelims for books

Plan prelims (the pages preceding the text) with care. Start a fresh folio for each; include a few (not all!) of the following:

Suggested copy for jacket or cover

Series title

List of other books in the same series or by the same author

Half title (see Prelim B of this manual)

Frontispiece: at this stage merely a folio headed

Frontispiece, see separate artwork to follow

Title page, including name of author with any decorations or degrees to be printed

Copy to follow (for Publisher's details, and copyright notice)

Dedication (To . . .); Epigraph (philosophical quotation)

Foreword, not written by the author

Preface, which may include acknowledgements

Acknowledgements

List of contents

Lists of illustrations, plates, maps, tables, in-text figures

List of abbreviations

Introduction

General map

Some prelim pages may be given a typed heading but at this stage otherwise left blank; all those finally intended must be included. Mark prelim folios A, B, C, etc., with the last one so marked. For a list of illustrations the copy will consist of numbered short titles or short summaries of captions. See 5.3.

Keep prelims for reports, catalogues and booklets very simple.

[A] 1.4 Final checking

After the prelims comes the main text. Folios must be typed <u>on one side only</u>. The text may be followed by some of these:

- Conclusion or epilogue
- Appendix or appendices
- Chronological table(s)
- Endnotes (see 3.4)
- Glossary
- Bibliography (see 3.5)
- Index (see 3.6)

There is no disgrace if occasional minor deletions or hand-written additions appear ~~show~~ in the ~~XXXXXXXXX~~ typescript, as long as they are clear, and fewer than in this demonstration paragraph. Try to make any amendments to the typescript clear <u>without</u> using marginal marks. Never amend in pencil. Use ink, or opaque white correcting fluid. All three copies of the typescript must be made to correspond.

Check and re-check cross-references to figure numbers and other books: check <u>original</u> sources (your quoted source may have its own errors). When the typescript is complete, number each folio, starting after the prelims with (1). A rubber stamp may be used to put the title of the work in the lower corner of each folio. Incorporate any last-minute amendments in all three copies with great care.

Whole folios of late additional material may be added, after (say) folio (60). First, <u>re-number</u> (60) as (60a); then add (60b), (60c), etc. Folio (59) must also be marked thus: [(59) 60 a–c follow].

Draw a line thus if a folio stops short, where copy on next folio is intended to follow on <u>without</u> a break.

Write (run on) if this happens in mid-sentence.

Never add extra paragraphs by means of hinged flaps. Instead, make any necessary partial deletion, and add a whole new folio; or re-type short alterations on smaller pieces of paper and paste them down all over the faulty passages. Try using white gummed paper.

If you remove a numbered folio because for good reason you wish to omit it altogether, a fruitless search for it will be set up by the publisher and printer. So, delete the page boldly and leave it in place, or replace it with a numbered blank. Write any notes to the printer (not for publication) in the margin, encircled, e.g. as p. 00 (folio 67).

The master typescript, plus two carbons or photocopies of the whole, now absolutely final and not liable to afterthoughts, should be made up into packets about an inch thick. For safety, list the inventory (see Prelim A of this manual) on each packet, with your name and address. Hole-punch the packets in the top left-hand corner, and thread each on to a tag; the reason for this is given on p. 00 (folio 65). Thus, packets of typescript should never be stapled, pinned, or glued together, or bound up as a book.

Never paste illustrations into your typescript. Your publisher may prefer to omit them altogether, for economic reasons. So try to plan your typescript on this basis; consult the publisher; see 5.1.

Where part of the copy is to follow later, incorporate a headed and numbered folio inscribed (Copy to follow). Copy for the index may be in this category. Send the two clearest copies of the typescript to the publisher; he will send one to the printer for keyboarding (typesetting) the text, and retain the other. You the author will keep the third copy.

If you are asked to incorporate changes, mark small alterations in a distinctive colour, and re-type large ones; list the folios affected so that the publisher can check them.

O

A —

1.5 Dealing with publishers and printers

(8)

The author who publishes on his own may encounter difficulties over copyright or libel. If you approach a publisher, you may be asked to consider a change of title, so as to reach a wider market, and to study a booklet giving advice on proof-correcting, copyright, libel, availability of bold type or small capitals (illustrated on p. 00) (folio 65), reproduction of illustrations, charges for corrections, and so on.

If you wish to include quotations or extracts from copyright works, seek advice on the legal complications from the publisher. You may be represented by a literary agent; this often helps.

Having accepted the two best copies of your finally-polished typescript, and agreed terms, the publisher's staff will 'mark up' one copy with detailed instructions for printing, ready to be keyboarded for conversion to a printed image by one of several methods. A staff typographic designer may be involved.

Correct proofs carefully, using the correct colour (ask the publisher), and return them promptly. Printers always have tight schedules and cannot keep promises of completion if you delay proofs. Authors who 're-write the book' at proof stage are regarded as criminals. Even changing one word at this stage may cost several pounds. Beware of exceeding your 'free' correction allowance. If a wrong (say) seven-letter word is found in proofs, try to replace it with another word of seven (or six) letters. This will save shifting all the type for some way ahead, and will eliminate the risk of further errors arising. Any queries raised by the printer's reader are not impertinent, and must be answered clearly. The publisher's designer may direct the planning and arrangement of the pages.

(Note to editors and designers: see also 4.6.)

2 Basic typing for print

2.1 Underlining; word-breaks

To the printer, any underlining you put in your typescript will mean: 'Please set in italic (sloping) type'. Therefore *never* underline except where italic is specifically required. Words not underlined are described as 'roman', i.e. normal or upright.

Italic provides distinction or emphasis; it may also be used for foreign words, quotations from manuscript, verse quotations, etc.; if over-used it appears pretentious. Italic may also be used for the words of one of the speakers in a dialogue, e.g. a lengthy reported interview. If words requiring italic appear in a sentence already in italic, type those words in roman, as in this extract from a manuscript diary. Friday 1 May: *Have just read the review in* The Times. *This evening at Meiringen, tried* fondue *with M. and C. Y.: an* amusing *business*. . . . (If underlining has to be removed, use typists' opaque white correcting fluid.)

Keep lines of typescript as even in length as possible, except that, to avoid misleading the printer, ensure that a hyphen *never* comes at the end (or beginning) of a line. Otherwise, a word like typescript may be printed with the unnecessary hyphen retained, thus:

> A word like type-script may be printed
> with the unnecessary hyphen retained.

To prevent this fault, carry over the whole word to the next line.

A few printers' terms will be used in this manual. See p. 00. Lower case means small letters as distinct from caps (capitals); a rule is a printed line or dash; a full point is a full stop; the sign # means 'space' in the U.K.; a solidus is a oblique stroke /.

2.2 Typing hyphens and dashes

What we call hi-fi quality recording was unknown, at the time of the Great War of 1914--18. Jack was already -- unknown to me -- dreaming of it when he said: 'Oh, d--- this machine! I wish I ---'

The above paragraph was written to show the four kinds of 'dash' used in printed English. The printer has all four sorts, as shown in section 1 of Fig. 2, p. 00. Each has a different meaning, so we must (even in typing) indicate clearly which is required.

The <u>hyphen</u> (see 2.5) joins words, and is typed unspaced: hi-fi, long-term, gilt-edged, system-built, rule-of-thumb decisions, tailor-made. It can also sustain a drawl: a hesitant 'Ye-e-es'.

A <u>span</u> of any kind, e.g. 1914--18, or the London--Dover road, is shown in print by a mark which is slightly wider than a hyphen. This span-mark (printers call it an en rule: see section 1 on p. 00) has to be represented in typescript by an unspaced double hyphen; any span, differentiation, or series is thus shown: pages 43--54; we won 3--0; rebuilt by Wren 1677--85; the World War 1939--45; a Liberal--Tory coalition; lines 23--39; the Berlin--Paris express; north--south routes; boy--girl friendships; 6--7 ft; red--green colourblind (but grey-green if greyish green); Anglo--Soviet relations. Consider also: the Alsace-Lorraine--Paris road, and 18th--20th-century art, where both span-mark <u>and</u> hyphen are required. (See also 'En rule', p. 00.)

The <u>dash</u> indicates a pause or break. Show it in typescript -- as here -- by a spaced double hyphen. Down -- still unceasingly -- still inevitably down! (<u>The pit and the pendulum.</u>) And: '. . . until I have -- blown to fragments -- the -- a -- detestable -- serpent -- HEEP! . . .' (<u>David Copperfield.</u>) And also -- unknown to me -- etc. But for neatness authors will often, as <u>here</u>, use commas, not dashes.

The long dash, very familiar to readers of nineteenth-century fiction, expresses an omitted word or part of a word, or an abruptly unfinished sentence. It is typed as a treble hyphen, spaced according to sense, as follows. Old W--- was a little, busy, cringing tradesman. (Essays of Elia.) 'Think, ma'am,' I rapturously began, 'oh---!' (David Copperfield.) Also: 'Oh, d--- this machine! I wish I ---'

A 2.3 Other punctuation

Punctuation is intended to aid understanding and to assist in reading aloud, by providing a guide to necessary pauses, emphasis, and changing inflection. Space your punctuation as in this manual.

Apostrophes. Jack's telephone, Joan Tyler's books. Charles's car, Dickens's works, at the Joneses' house, St James's Square, Rabelais's works. But type with terminal apostrophe: for goodness' sake, Moses' law, Jesus' words, and (classical names) Ceres' rites, Mars' armour. No possessive apostrophe appears in Reuters Ltd, Earls Court, Golders Green, St Albans, St Andrews, St Davids, St Helens, St Ives, St Neots or St Leonards: nor of course in possessives hers, ours, theirs, yours, its. The book lacked its cover, but it's a fine day (elision). Do not type an apostrophe before phone, plane, bus, cello. Decades: in the thirties of the century. But type an apostrophe in '74 and '75, and special plural forms: do's and dont's, two f's in paraffin, etc. Aren't, isn't, I'll, we'll, don't, can't, she's and it's (it is or it has) are all typed without a space before or after the apostrophe.

Colon. Never put a dash after the colon when introducing a list with the words as follows: (The colon alone is enough.)

Quotation marks: for direct speech and odd quoted words, many publishers regard 'single quotes' as neater than "double quotes". With single quotation marks, double are used for quotes within quotes, e.g. He replied: 'Tom surprised her by saying "It's all done, aunt."' Note that a quotation mark is never typed above a full point, unless it is meant to be read as an exclamation mark!

The order of punctuation marks should be according to sense. But complications arise, especially over the position of the terminal point, when it coincides with the end of a quotation. Put the point right at the end when the quoted part (whether spoken or not) is a relatively minor part of the whole sentence. This rule operates in the first two examples, where the short quoted phrase needs no terminal point, but where the main sentence does need one:

None can be identified as the 'best buy'.

What do we mean by 'romantic'?

He exclaimed: 'Please don't use that word "romantic"!'

She said: 'I suppose you'll come on a number 63 bus.'

He replied: 'I've made no plans. I'll decide after I "unwind".'

The last two examples show the point inside, the quoted phrase being the major part of the whole sentence. Even when the quoted words make a complete sentence, they may have to be denied a terminal point within the quotation marks if the main sentence continues immediately:

When he said 'It's all done, aunt', Tom Sawyer really meant it.

Tom said, 'It's all done, aunt': but she did not believe him.

When Tom said 'It's all done, aunt' she did not believe him.

When a quotation is interrupted at a point where a pause occurred in what was actually said, a comma goes inside the quotation marks. Where there was no such pause, the comma is outside the quotation marks. The encircled comma is the relevant one:

'Yes,' said Tom, 'she's awful particular about this fence.'

'Yes, she's awful particular', said Tom, 'about this fence.'

Omit commas if you can: 'What' asked Lloyd George 'is our task?'

Question marks, exclamation marks. Pedantic accuracy requires two such marks in the first example below, but most writers would make one mark do the duty of two (second example). The third example is difficult because one can hardly exclaim and question at the same time.

He questioned me. 'Didn't I ask "Do you know that man?"?'

He questioned me. 'Didn't I ask "Do you know that man?"'

He asked: 'Did Laura say "I am so helpless!"?'

She echoed him: 'She did indeed say "I am so helpless!"'

Ellipsis. For words omitted in mid-sentence . . . three spaced points are typed. . . . Note that in the latter example the previous sentence ended with its own full point, preceding the ellipsis.

Parentheses and square brackets. Both kinds are often required in printed work. Draw square brackets by hand if they cannot be typed properly. Square brackets, not parentheses, are used when the author or editor is inserting a comment or explanatory phrase within any extract, especially an extract from a copyright work (see 3.1):

Then, disaster: in June, my personal aide [Col Xyz of MN6, a notorious rogue] defaulted.

But moil [labour hard] not too much under ground (Bacon, Essays, 1625).

I assure you that the early tapes will reveal nothing [italics not in original -- Ed.]

We, the undersigned [i.e. all the staff except Jones] now request to be transferred.

Gladstone and Disreali [sic] have disagreed.

Parentheses may be used (as here) for a parenthetical phrase. But parentheses as above may often be replaced by commas, as here, in order to minimize interruption of reading. Simplify. Parentheses can often be omitted thus and may not even require commas instead.

Systems jargon. Post codes, STD phone numbers, and indeed many other systems have their own rules for spaces, points and hyphens, which should be observed. For instance, a London phone number might be 01-242 1655, with only one hyphen as shown.

The solidus. The solidus or oblique stroke in 1975/76 indicates a financial year, football season, or similar definite period; 1975--76 is vaguer and may be as much as two whole years. Avoid using the term and/or; this is jargon borrowed from forms, where the citizen is asked to state his/her preference, or answer yes/no. The same sense of alternatives underlies the use of the solidus in an on/off switch, or a drive-on/drive-off ferryboat. It represents division in fractions such as 1/100 000, to avoid using the clumsy form $\frac{1}{100\ 000}$, but for map scales the style 1:100 000 is better.

The comma. Omit unnecessary commas. But a comma can be important; check copy for ambiguities. Compare the following as regards sense: However we may reject . . . / However, we may reject . . .

A comma is needed in the middle of this sentence: after the Treaty of Versailles Alsace and Lorraine became part of France. The insertion of two commas could reverse the sense of: Sir Thomas Atkins said Charles Smith has now retired.

Type references to groups as black, white, and green, rather than as black, white and green, if there is any risk of incorrectly suggesting that some are black, while others might be striped white and green. The second comma is sometimes also necessary with alternatives: black, white, or green.

2.4 Spelling

Consistency is required in each book or series, but is difficult to achieve. Do we spell standard<u>ize</u>, standard<u>ization</u>, or standardise, standardisation? The publisher may insist on -ize, or he may allow you if you wish to spell -ise. Oxford University Press always spell standardize, criticize, etc.; this way, we have to list the words which for etymological reasons we <u>must</u> always spell with an <u>s</u>. These are: advertise, advise, affranchise, apprise (inform), arise, braise, chastise, circumcise, comprise, compromise, demise, despise, devise, disfranchise, disguise, emprise, enfranchise, enterprise, excise, exercise, expertise, franchise, improvise, incise, merchandise, premise (verb), prise (force open), reprise, revise, seise (in law), supervise, surmise, surprise, televise, treatise, and words in -yse like analyse, paralyse. This list must be memor<u>ized</u> by -<u>izers</u>.

Some fortunate persons find spelling easy; others have to make a conscious effort to achieve the correct modern form of channelled, paralleled, focused, unbiased, flyable, blameable, harass, losable, complement, defensible, exorbitant, manoeuvre, octopuses, cargoes, fiascos, minuscule, and disparate. Compare practise and practice; affect, effect; stationery, stationary; practical, practicable; forbear, forebear; forgo, forego; principle, principal; dependent, dependant; and siege, seize, gauge; unmistakable but unshakeable; battalion, accommodate, desiccation, millennium.
Names: see 6.1. Look for wrong variant names (e.g. the same person as James McLean/Maclean/MacLean), and check plurals of Latin words used in English. When correcting proofs, remember that the printer may have set causal as casual, deprecate as depreciate, principal as principle, risible as visible, consensus as concensus, uninformed as

uniformed, -tive as -tion and vice versa, etc. Avoid diphthongs ae and oe: spell medieval, primeval, ecumenical, phoenix, archaeology, palaeography. But *French* oeuf etc. American spellings: see p. 00.

2.5 When to hyphenate

Words gradually coalesce; down-stairs and to-day in Dickens are now downstairs and today. Avoid using hyphens if possible, either by keeping the words apart or by joining them together. Sense may however *require* a hyphen, which must be put in the right place. A fine tooth-comb needs a hyphen, but should read a fine-tooth comb. (We do not comb our teeth.) If a necessary hyphen is omitted, the tailor-made dresses would change meaning, and a man-eating tiger becomes ridiculous. Hi-fi is acceptable current jargon.

General principles apply. A house may be built of red brick, but we often save time and space and say a red-brick house. An actor is well known, but we write a well-known actor with a hyphen; likewise the records are out of date, but out-of-date records, and a ton of cast iron, but a cast-iron pillar. A-level, long-term and law-abiding are hardly intelligible without a hyphen. Hyphens are vital in distinguishing twenty-two-ton lorries from twenty two-ton lorries, and extra-official hours from extra official hours. Hyphens also prevent awkward accidents of juxtaposition: co-respondent, not corespondent; teach-in and work-in, not teachin and workin; re-run and re-elect, not rerun and reelect; Inverness-shire, not Invernessshire. The hyphen is used in spelt-out fractions, times, and decades: a half-dozen, two-thirds, forty-seven sixty-fourths, half-past eight, the eighteen-forties; and in Sub-Lieutenant, etc. Some French christian names and places in France have hyphens: Jean-Paul Sartre, Saint-Jean-de-Luz.

But nowadays we often join words: motorway, paperback, reopen, coeducational, radioactive, horsepower, oncoming, airline, fourfold, midday, sightseeing, subcommittee, thermonuclear, antifreeze, daytime, logbook, lopsided, nonstop, setback, and wallpaper.

Some words should be kept apart: half a dozen, half an hour, hue and cry, in so far, every one of them (but everyone agrees). There is no need to hyphenate or join up familiar phrases like mulberry bush, milk bottle, paving stone, or vacuum cleaner.

A 2.6 Use of capitals

A capital letter creates specific sense for an otherwise general term: a government building, but a Government decision at top level; any speaker, any house, but the Speaker of the House (of Commons). A capital is used to indicate a title, proper name, or group name: Mr Jack Grey, Sir Henry Green; the Crown; the President of the United States; a Proclamation, the Bar, the Cabinet, the Church; also for abbreviations of titles: a K.C.M.G., an M.B.E.; for races: the Anglo-Saxons, Negroes, Aborigines; for names of administrative areas, both formal and informal: England, New England; groups and companies and their members: the Labour Party, a Liberal, a Methodist; proper names given to events and objects: May Day, the Palace of Westminster, the Mona Lisa; currently-registered trade names: Decca, Hoover, Xerox, Pyrex, Shell, Vaseline, Monotype; and names of hotels:

at the Royal Oak, but in quotes to prevent ambiguity: at 'The Castle', at 'The Inn on the Park'. Some adjectives are capitalized: the Victorian era, Indian art.

Capitals are used for pronouns referring to the Deity, but not for associated relative pronouns who, which, that. Formally, The Queen is so capitalized, also She, Her Majesty, Their Royal Highnesses, but when informal style as: the Queen left her car.

Italic is used for references to published books, very long poems, periodicals, plays, films, ships, and (in military history) enemy formations: Tolstoy's *Anna Karenina*, Dickens's *Bleak House*, Milton's *Paradise Lost*; *The Times*, *The Economist*, *The Scotsman*, but for other papers lower case 'the': the *Daily Mail*, the *New Statesman*; *The Mousetrap*, *1 Henry IV*, Orson Welles's *Citizen Kane*; Nelson's *Victory*, *Gipsy Moth*; the *28th Army*. Do not italicize a possessive *s*; type thus: the *Mona Lisa*'s smile. But type in roman: the Bible; Genesis and all other books of the Bible; the Koran; titles of Acts of Parliament; names of trains and types of ship, car or aircraft: the Finance Act 1973, the Brighton Belle, a Dreadnought, a Zodiac, a Silver Cloud, a Boeing. Style classes of locomotives thus: 'King Arthur' class, but italicize individual locomotives, aircraft, and ships: the driver of *Sir Menadeuke*, the crew of the *Graf Zeppelin*, the *R 101*, H.M.S. *Victory*. Style radio and television programmes thus: 'Panorama', 'Woman's Hour'. See study list at 6.1.

Type managing director, the board, and committee without capitals if possible; Managing Director, Board, and Committee can look pompous.

Lower case is used for vague or general references: every country has a head of state; every American school and company has a president; titles like sir, madam, monsignor (but capitalized when formal, or when attached to the name, e.g. I said to Sir Charles: 'Yes, sir.')

Names of regions: northern England and eastern Australia (vague) but Northern Ireland and Western Australia; a renaissance of folk-art but the Italian Renaissance; pre-war, post-war, and verbal war between parties, but the Great War 1914--18; liberal-minded people but the Liberal Party; democratic ideas but the Democrats; a local post office but the Post Office as a whole; socialism, surrealism, conservatism and other -isms; the world, the sun, the moon, north, south, east, west, summer, autumn, winter, and spring.

Use lower case also for words originally taken from names: arabic numeral, asian flu, china tea, christian name, french polish, indian corn, indian ink, indiarubber, macadamize, machiavellian, morocco leather, plaster of paris, platonic, prussian blue, roman type, satanic, scotch and soda, socratic, spenserian, venetian blind.

A → 2.7 Abbreviations

Typing full points after all shortened words gives a very 'dotty' effect, e.g. Mr. and Mrs. Grey. So, for simple text, put a full point after abbreviations, where the end of the word is cut off, e.g. Prof., B.C. etc.; but omit the point with contractions, where the first and last letters remain, as Mr Mrs Messrs Dr Revd and so on.

For more scholarly work, use the following three-stage method, which will assist you in achieving consistent modern style.

Stage 1: practice: always omit full points for terms in this 'common list': Mr Mrs Messrs Dr Revd Bt St, French titles Mme Mmes Mlle Mlles Mgr Ste; the well-known terms BBC EEC IOU ITV MP SOS TV; Alf Di etc.; hi-fi pub flu vet exam intercom bra lab prep; Co Ltd, per cent, revs per minute; £E $A hr ft cwt lb p (decimal pence) and lbw; metric (SI) units such as g cm km; C Cd Cmd Cmnd (series of Command Papers); also mv (motor vessel) and ss (screw steamer). Further, omit the point from acronyms, i.e. pronounceable groups of initials e.g. NATO Unesco UNICEF; and short forms e.g. Pan Am Co-op and Oxfam. The spoken usage would make full points seem wrong. Form plurals (without apostrophe) MPs IOUs hrs; plurals without s: ft cwt lb p and all metric (SI) units such as cm m km g kg.

Stage 2: your own 'omit points' list. Consult your publisher; he may have strong views. Then compile your short list, additional to the common list above, of terms used in your own specialism, from which you intend to omit full points. Fowler/Gowers Modern English usage p. 445 sanctions 'no points' for all contractions; historians may list AD BC USSR etc.; architects may list RIBA etc.; chess experts may list Kt KRP etc.; technologists may list min sec oz yd in (inch) ADP LPG etc.; see 4.2. In non-technical work, symbols may be listed, and may be given plural s: yds ins; others take no s: g cm min sec oz etc. Do not list honours or qualifications: see 'Names', below.

Stage 3: retain full points with all others which are not on the common list or your own list. You may retain points in i.e. e.g. etc. a.m. p.m. viz. no. nos. and French titles M., MM. Form plurals without apostrophe: N.C.O.s yds. ins.; some without s: min. sec. oz.

Names: initials are spaced; abbreviations for honours, decorations and qualifications are shown (in that order) with full points but unspaced between the letters, as in these examples:

J. B. Grey, C.B.E., F.R.Hist.S.

Prof. Sir Henry Green, Ph.D.(London), F.R.S.A.

R. S. Black, C.Eng., F.I.Mech.E., F.R.S.H., R.E.(Retd.)

A. P. Brown, D.S.C., D.Sc., F.R.I.C.

Names etc. so typed may be printed by the publisher as he wishes with *or* without full points, or with small capitals, thus: J. B. Grey, C.B.E.

The above system should enable you to achieve acceptable and consistent treatment in your typescript. There may be occasional problems: *an* R.A.F. uniform, while spoken usage suggests *a* RAF-type moustache to go with it. See also 4.6. Some firms with double names use the & (ampersand) sign: Secker & Warburg; others do not: Thames and Hudson. If in doubt, spell out. Never type &c for etc.

Over-use of abbreviations may annoy the reader. But an abbreviation introduced at the first opportunity may be used thereafter to save space, thus: . . . the Oxford English Dictionary (O.E.D.) was the parent . . . and . . . thus the O.E.D. became the . . . etc.

Use lower case when there is no reason for capitals.

To help the general reader, you may give a *list of abbreviations* and their meanings in the prelims.

A

2.8 Foreign words

'*Ja*, Cornelis,' said Peter Pienaar on page 52 of *Greenmantle*; the word is in italic because it is not commonly used in English. But façade, fiancée and fête are anglicized and so do not require italic. Type whole sentences of foreign dialogue in roman: 'Hé! bonjour, monsieur!' said the fox, 'Que vous êtes joli!' Draw accents neatly in ink.

If extra words are to be inserted, make it clear whether they are to be closed up: Quid quid agunt homines might be typeset wrongly as Quid quid agunt homines. So amend thus: ~~Quid~~ Quidquid agunt homines.

There is unfortunately no law to restrain authors from showing off by using too many odd foreign phrases. The typist may therefore practise the study lists at the end of this manual. List 6.3 shows that some words e.g. amour propre may be typed in roman in fiction or popular periodicals, but should be underlined for italic in serious work and reference books: *amour propre*, etc. Other foreign words (list 6.4) are not anglicized and should always be underlined for italic: *jeu d'esprit*, *coup d'oeil*; note special diphthong marking.

A date typed in English as 13 May 1974 would in French have the month in lower case as 13 mai 1974; in German thus: 13. Mai 1974.

2.9 Numbers, times, dates

210 books were found in the box. Beginning with figures looks wrong, so re-write: Two hundred and ten books were found in the box; or: In the box were found 210 books.

Which numbers are spelt out in full? There are three methods. Generally, for *fiction and descriptive writing* type as follows: in his eightieth year; seventeen men climbed up; eight per cent interest; four hundred ships sank; ten thousand horses; it was fifteen below zero; at ten in the morning; at noon; at four-thirty in the afternoon; the train left at 5.39; on the first of May 1974; 13 May 1974; 143 High Street, Southwark. Spell out vague amounts: three or four miles. Use figures for scores in games: they won 3--0. Dates in speech: 'We left on 1 May and reached Madrid on the 23rd.'

But for *historical works and serious reference books* type those phrases with numerals only where statistical: in his eightieth year; seventeen men climbed up; 8 per cent interest; 400 ships sank; 10,000 horses; it was 15 degrees below zero; at ten a.m.; at 12 noon; at 4.30 p.m.; the train left at 5.39 (or 17.39); on 1 May 1974; 13 May 1974; 143 High Street, London SE1 2BN. Spell out isolated numbers one to ninety-nine; use figures for most of the rest. But be consistent: 17 prisoners marched with 1400 soldiers, *not* seventeen with 1400.

For *technical books*, go still further with use of numerals: 8% interest, minus 15°C, at 10 a.m. or 1000 hours, 12 noon or 1200 hours, etc. With the 24-hour clock, the day begins at 0000 hours, morning ends at 1159 hours, afternoon begins at 1200 hours, and the day ends at 2359 hours. See also 4.2 for treatment of technical text. Do not use the term billion: its meaning varies (U.S.A. and U.K. differ).

Decimal point: as 0.5 (British Standard) or centred as 0·5.

Prices: British: £2.30 30p 10½p £2.30½ (no full point after p; *not* as £2.30p or £0.10½p). American: $125.75, but $125 if there are no cents; *not* $125.00. French: 125.75 fr.; West German: DM 125.75.

Mark differentiation between l and 1 or 1, and between 0 and O; three *l*'s in parallel; post code FY0 1YN; he drew a round O.

Roman numerals: Henry VIII, Elizabeth II, Pope John XXIII; not VIIIth, IInd, and not VIII., II., etc. Never type 1 for I or vice versa: II is roman two but 11 is arabic eleven.

Large numbers: type commas in 1,234,567 (in mathematics or science, style 1 234 567); no comma in large page, line or house numbers: page 1234, line 1234, 1234 Six Mile Drive, Long Beach.

Years: 1974/5 for a financial year or football season; 1974--75 is a vague period over two years. Decades: the 1970s, 1980s. In '74, '75. Between 1801--9 *and* from 1801--9 are *wrong*; type thus: between 1801 and 1809, from 1801 to 1809, or simply 1801--9. Type A.D. 300, and A.D. 1975, but note that B.C. follows figures: 10,000 B.C. (comma only if five figures or more). For spans use minimum figures; reading aloud tells us the minimum required: 1801--9, 1970--74, 1736--38, 1870--1906. Dates B.C. are ambiguous if abbreviated, so type as 257--251 B.C., not 257--51 B.C. or 257--1 B.C.

Dates: Monday 13 May 1974, not Monday, 13th May, 1974 or Monday May 13th, 1974. The all-figure style in the U.K. is 13.5.1974, but in U.S.A. it is month first, as 5.13.1974. The international all-figure style is year, month, day: 1974-05-13, or 1974 05 13, or 19740513.

A 2.10 Headings

Type headings flush left as in this manual. They may not need numbers. Mark all Chapters (1, 2 etc.) as (Chap), and subheadings as [A], [B]. (Parts I, II etc., each containing several Chapters, would be marked (Part Title).) Keep headings short: one long heading can ruin the appearance of a book when printed. Use minimum capitalization: Headings Thus Look Pompous; but note capitals necessary and intended: The King sends for More [Sir Thomas More]; A Conservative view [political, not general]; I form a Great Resolution [mock-heroic]. Show spans in full: The year 1801 to 1809, not 1801--9. Never type headings in capitals, or underlined, or with a terminal full point. You may discuss printing style, type size, spacing, centred or flush left etc. with your publisher's professional designer; or leave these matters to him. He can convert easily the style shown in this manual.

Subsubheadings may be underlined and run on, as at 3.4. Numbering systems for lists or subsections (a, b, c broken down to i, ii, iii and 1, 2, 3; or 1, 1.1, 1.1.1, 1.2, 1.2.1 etc.), if necessary, must be typed with consistent indention, wherever you employ them.

O

Chap 3 Systematic treatment of details

A 3.1 Quotations in text

Short quotations are run on 'in quotes' in the text. Whatever the oddities of spelling and style, copy the original with care, including even old usage of letters (I haue vnderstoode); a long s should not be typed f but drawn in thus: almoſt. (Print old long s) Peculiar features may be followed by [sic] meaning 'it was thus in the original'. Editorial explanations may also be put in square brackets: 'But moil [labour hard] not too much under ground' (Bacon, Essays, 1625). See 2.3. Parts of copyright works must not be copied without permission.

A 3.2 Extracts

As a rule, a quotation in English of less than fifty words or so would be shown run-on in quotes in the text, but if longer may be set out as an extract, to be printed either in smaller type or indented. The following is typed as if it were an extract from another work:

> Indent the whole extract five spaces, starting flush left. Start subsequent paragraphs with extra indent, as follows.
>
> Any quoted passage in a foreign language, if at least a whole sentence, may be arranged as an extract, preferably in roman, not italic. At the end of an extract, the source may be given, as follows. (Author, Title, etc.)
>
> Or as follows. -- Author, Title, etc.

Recommence main text flush left, as here, if the sense runs straight on from the extract; otherwise, recommence the text style with a normal three-space paragraph indent.

A long extract of direct speech (i.e. actual spoken words within quotation marks) may run to more than one paragraph. If so, each paragraph should start with a quotation mark, but only the last paragraph has one at the end.

Quoted passages of verse should reproduce with care the poet's capitalization and indention scheme. A photostat of the original is ideal as copy. Short verse quotations may be in text, using the solidus to indicate a line break, thus: 'Come; we have no friend/ But resolution,' (*Antony and Cleopatra*.) *Or*, set as an extract, starting as in the original:

> Come; we have no friend
> But resolution,

in which case quotation marks are not used. Note how a letter *e*, normally mute, may in verse be marked è when it is to be pronounced: 'Hence, loathèd melancholy!' For copyright problems, see 1.5.

Quoted passages in a foreign language may be marked (Verse) or (Prose) in the side margin, to assist the printer.

3.3 Terminology for notes

If you are writing a scholarly text, you may wish to add further details and sources of information, in the form of footnotes. We might lead the reader's eye from the relevant point in the text to the note by using an indicator symbol thus* or a superior figure thus[1]; the note may be on the same page or elsewhere. Several systems are in common use: pros and cons of these systems are listed at 3.4.

See p. 0 for method of referring the reader to another page. Authors should also refer to Collins or Butcher (books listed on p. 00) in order to achieve consistent and correct usage of the Latin words and abbreviations which, in scholarly and learned works, are used to make notes compact: c., cf., e.g., et al., etc., fl., ibid., id., i.e., loc. cit., MS., N.B., op. cit., passim, P.S., q.v., sic, s.v., v., viz. (passim and sic have no full point). Abbreviations directing the reader to parts of a book are: app., b. or bk., c. or ch., f. (plural ff.), fig., fn. (plural fnn.), fol., n. (plural nn.), p. (plural pp.), para., pl., sec., ser., suppl., vol., etc.

The word *line* is best spelt out, as l. is easily confused with arabic figure 1, likewise *verse*, as v. can mean *volume* or lower case roman five. Use ed. for edited or editor, and edn. for edition.

The parts of the book may be capitalized App., Bk., etc. when referring to another part of your own work. Underline for italic such directions to the reader as *continued*, *see also*, *for* Gray *read* Grey, and for pinpointing letters e.g. the *ae* in orthopaedic. Type in quotation marks the titles of short stories which are parts of the book: 'The spectacles' in Poe's *Tales of mystery and imagination*.

Lower case is neat for roman figures: scene iii, or vol. xxxviii.

3.4 Recommended systems for notes

Copious footnotes are extremely costly to set in type and make up into pages; they also create a somewhat pedantic visual effect, or annoy the reader by forcing him to break off reading to find a note which may be of no interest to him. Recommended methods for providing notes are listed below in normal order of preference, having regard to the crucial costs of typesetting as well as to readability.

Merging notes into the text. 'Notes which are essential to the text should not be separated from it' (Hugh Williamson, Methods of book design, O.U.P., London, 1966). Where you can, go a stage further: incorporate your notes into the text itself, as for example the reference above to Williamson's book. The residue of note material, if any, may be treated by one of the following methods.

Occasional footnotes. One short footnote every ten or twenty pages, if essential, is unlikely to be refused by your publisher. Use an asterisk as indicator. Typing arrangement: see 'Footnotes', following.

Numbered chapter endnotes. Superior figures thus[1] in the text act as indicators to numbered notes printed together at the end of each chapter. (They tend to be difficult to find.) Start afresh in each chapter with figure [1]. Head copy thus: (Endnotes for Chapter 3).

Numbered endnotes. Superior figures in the text can act as indicators referring to numbered notes printed together at the end of the book. This is often the best system. The figures can run in one series all through the book, although three-figure numbers may look clumsy. Endnotes are uncomplicated to set in type, and do not have to be re-numbered when the pages are made up by the printer. Endnotes can be lengthy, without looking awkward.

Type endnote copy double spaced on separate folios at the end, headed (Copy for endnotes). The superior figures in text may appear after the relevant word thus[33] or at the end of the sentence, after a full point, thus.[34] For style details, see footnote 1 under 'Footnotes', following. Problems may arise with incorporating late alterations, especially if numbering is affected.

Side-notes in margins and cut-in notes must especially be avoided.

Footnotes in large numbers are awkward; they will add to the production time of the book -- and to its price. (The printer has to separate footnote copy from the text copy, and set it in smaller type. He then has to assemble the text type in portions for pages, leaving room for the relevant footnote type, which also has to be broken into portions. Correct reference figures or symbols then have to be inserted in both text and notes. Time-consuming, expensive, and tedious to check. Alterations to numbering cause hideous confusion.)

If the publisher agrees to footnotes, start numbering afresh in each chapter with [1], and type the notes on separate folios headed e.g. Footnotes for Chapter 3. Or, type them all at foot of text folios, as below. Reduce the number of notes by combining them. For rare single notes, use an asterisk, not a figure. Type references to books with care.[1] In footnotes on later pages referring again to a book or article, type in still shorter form: See Gowers, pp. 7--12; Monotype Recorder vol. 42 no. 4, p. 13. Abbreviate names of months, and books of the Bible, as 2 Chron. 18:11. If i.e. or e.g. begin a footnote, type them in lower case.[2] Never add footnotes to incorporate important late afterthoughts at proof stage. Put them into line-end spaces in the text. Use short words: pack in tightly. Count letters if need be.

---

[1] As an example, assume that we wish to refer the reader to Gowers's Plain words. The full bibliography style (as at 3.5) will mention HMSO as publisher, but the footnote will be in short form, i.e. See Gowers, The complete plain words, 1973, pp. 7--12. Or article in a periodical: Monotype Recorder, vol. 42 no. 4, 1963, p. 13.

[2] e.g. as here.

3.5 Reference lists

A *bibliography* is a list of all books and articles recommended to the reader for further study, often with comments. The list sequence may (as the specimen list below) be alphabetical by authors' names; there may be more than one list, each covering a special subject or chronological period. Some books listed will be referred to in the *text*, e.g. 'But Judith Butcher (1975) gives Cambridge usage as . . .'

A *reference list*, on the other hand, lists only books and articles actually referred to in the text; the order of the list may be that in which the text references occur. Each item is numbered, so Miss Butcher's book might be referred to in the *text* simply by the number thus: 'But Cambridge usage[1] is . . .' If superior figures are already in use for footnotes, style the figure as (1) or [1].

In scholarly works, a bibliography *or* a reference list may appear at the end of each chapter rather than at the end of the book.

Specimen *bibliography* entries follow; the books listed may be of interest to the typist and the author. Note flush-left typing with turnovers indented three spaces.

Butcher, J., *Copy-editing, the Cambridge handbook*, Cambridge University Press, 1975. Written for publishers' staff; but deals with matters which may worry the author, e.g. complications and details of style in works of a scholarly nature.

Collins, F. H., *Authors and printers dictionary*, 11th edn., Oxford University Press, London, 1973. Odd omission of apostrophes in the title. Otherwise reliable, and for everyday use. Gives a single recommended form for spellings, where dictionaries give confusing alternatives; also sound on all other style details.

Downie, R. A. (ed.), 'Languages of the world', The Monotype Recorder, vol. 42, no. 4, Monotype Corporation, (see below,) London, 1963.

Fowler, H. W. and F. G. (eds.), The concise Oxford dictionary of current English, 5th edn., rev. E. McIntosh, Clarendon Press, Oxford, 1964. Often referred to as the C.O.D. (Why do we spell sailor, not sailer? Endings have subtleties of meaning: see the alphabetical entries -er, -or, -ite, -ic, -ical, -ee, -ible, -ful, -ine, etc., and prefixes post-, pre-.)

Hart's rules for compositors and readers at the Oxford University Press, 37th edn., Oxford University Press, London, 1967.
A companion to Collins, over which it takes precedence.

Lockwood, A., Diagrams, Studio Vista, London, 1969. Shows a wide range of methods of presenting ideas graphically.

Monotype Corporation, now at Salfords, Redhill, Surrey: booklets (as available) on typefaces, printing mathematical work, etc.

Rees, H., Rules of printed English, Darton Longman and Todd, London, 1970. Useful guidance on details, and a list of American usage.

Roget, P.M., Thesaurus of English words and phrases, various edns.

Sellers, L., Keeping up the style, Pitman, London, 1974.
For journalists especially; entertaining and informative.

If you have to check American/English spellings, refer to one of the standard American--English dictionaries published by Wm. Collins, Longmans, Oxford University Press, etc. Apart from differing meanings, spelling pitfalls include color/colour, honor/honour etc.; analyze/analyse etc.; caliber/calibre, center/centre etc.; catalog/ catalogue; plow/plough; ax/axe; defense/defence etc.; traveler/ traveller; anemia/anaemia etc.; fulfill/fulfil etc.; woolen/woollen; license, practice are in English both -ce nouns but -se verbs.

Copies of British Standards are available from BSI, 2 Park Street, London W1A 2BS; they include the following relevant to our subject:

BS 5261 Copy preparation and proof correction (Part 1: 1975: Preparation of typescript copy for printing)

BS 1219: 1958 Proof correction (to be superseded by Part 2 of BS 5261 in due course)

BS 1629 Bibliographical references

BS 1749 Alphabetical arrangement

BS 1991 Letter symbols, signs and abbreviations

BS 2979 Transliteration of Cyrillic and Greek characters

BS 3700 Preparation of indexes for books, periodicals etc.

BS 3763 The international system of units (SI)

BS 4148 Abbreviation of titles of periodicals

BS 4280 Transliteration of Arabic characters

BS 4812 Romanization of Japanese

BS 4884 Specifications for technical manuals

BS 4754 Presentation of bibliographical information in printed music

BS 4755 Presentation of translations

In this manual we try to follow Hart, Collins, and BS 5261. On a few points they disagree. Modern English usage persuades us to join up (not hyphenate) antifreeze, daytime, logbook, lopsided, nonstop, setback, and wallpaper. We also suggest when to type in roman instead of italic for foreign words, in study list 6.3. It is possible that BS 5261 Part 1 may seem indecisive, where it attempts to indicate the variant practices common in publishing, without recommending one as against the other, e.g. the use or non-use of full points after contractions. If this manual also seems a little conservative in such details of style, remember that any publisher's staff can easily mark deletion of excessive detail in copy, if they have to; but it is not so easy for them to find space to mark insertions, where they have to amend copy which the publisher finds unacceptably 'modern'. If authors, publishers, designers and printers eventually come to agree on further stages of standardization, the labours of all concerned will become a little lighter.

A — 3.6 Preparing an index

A non-fiction book usually deserves a good analytical index, compiled either by the author or by a professional indexer with the author's help. (This book, being merely a manual for practice, has no index.) References in an index are normally to page numbers, which are not known until after the printer has made up the pages. Index finalization therefore comes at a very late stage of production: printing is held up if the index is delayed. If on the other hand there are section numbers or paragraph numbers, the index references can be to these, so that the index can be finalized along with the original typescript. Consult your publisher at an early stage.

One combined index is usually better than several indexes covering various aspects in turn. All spelling in the index must be as in the text. While compiling entries, the indexer may notice apparent errors in the text, which he will rightly query. An index may be headed with a note, as follows.

References are to page numbers, with main entries in bold figures thus: 23. References to figures are in italic: 24, and to plates, in roman figures: XXV.

The first index-entry example above shows typing in turnover indent style (which can also be used to present examples in textbooks and manuals: for such examples in this manual, see the sentences using square brackets on p. 00 (folio 13); also pp. 0, 00, 00, 00, 00, and 00 (folios 5 30 31 32 42 50)).

An alternative typing style for index entries (less economical of space) starts on a fresh indented line for each sub-entry, with additional indent and fresh line for any sub-sub-entries.

The typist should check which alphabetical order system is intended, before checking the order itself. The letter-by-letter system suns as: W., water, Waterford, water-mills, waterproofing, water systems, water-wheels, W.B., etc. The word-by-word system runs as: W., W.B., water, water-mills, water systems, water-wheels, Waterford, waterproofing. Hyphens are treated as spaces. This is not an easy subject: see BS 3700.

An index on cards, with one entry on each card, may be acceptable. Ask. Such cards should be uniform in size, legible, typed on one side only, and with marks ☐ or ☐☐ at the start of the relevant lines to indicate indenting for sub-entries. For obvious reasons, the cards should also be numbered in sequence.

O

A

3.7 Typographical complications

We opened the envelope; the message inside read thus: ПУШЕНЬЕ ЗАБРАНЬЕНО. Such strange characters may be a code message in a mystery novel, a casual phrase in modern Cyrillic, or a classical quotation in a learned work. Do not overlook the fact that obtaining type for such foreign characters can delay printing of the whole book for several weeks. Keep to the ordinary alphabet if possible. If such material is essential, in some cases you may find that you can bring various bits of it together so as to make a substantial diagram: dry-transfer alphabets can be used to create camera-ready copy for printing. See 5.4. Some expert authors will be able to transcribe words in an exotic language into the ordinary roman alphabet, which is an even simpler solution of the problem.

See illustration at p. 00 (folio 65) of this manual, which shows that there are two kinds of arabic figures: old style, to go with lower case and small caps, and lining figures, which align with capitals. Only one kind will normally be used throughout a book. The publisher will advise. If you know for certain that small capitals and bold type will be available for your book, you may suggest to the publisher's design staff that such types might be used for specific purposes, taking care not to overdo them; you would mark copy THUS for small caps, thus for bold lower case, and THUS for bold caps. THIS would be printed as This.

Small capitals may be used, but only in conjunction with old style figures, for the following: for emphasizing names in reference books: KENSINGTON is . . . London SW7; follow the A436 road to NEWTOWN; for honours, degrees: J. B. Grey, C.B.E., F.R.Hist.S.; for beginning a formal letter (quoted as extract): MY DEAR SIR, and at the end: I remain very faithfully yours, ROBERT CLIVE (without terminal point); to reproduce the style of a telegram, as COME HOME ALL FORGIVEN STOP WATSON STOP; or as the words on a notice: the sign over the shop read GROCERY AND PR VISIONS, or signpost: FOLLY, PLUSH, MAPPOWDER, or placard: CABINET LEAK ROW. Also for references: Hamlet II i 30, Mark 1:14 RSV; and for organizations: OXFAM, UNESCO; post codes: London W1A 2BS; and for dates: 52 B.C., A.D. 500.

Bold type creates a spotty appearance (italic or small caps will usually look better for emphasis), but bold type can be used in moderation for run-on subheadings in reference books, as follows:

Bold subheadings thus would be printed same size as the text. Bold is likely to have special significance in scientific work. Bold italic is only rarely available. Do not demand it.

Displayed typography is often unnecessary: lists in the text can usually be typed not in columns but in simple run-on style: thus:

Chairman: Sir Alfred Adams, O.B.E.

Members: Arbuthnot B. Airey, Ministry of Documents
A. S. Ayling, Ministry of Documents
Andrew Anton, Consultant
A. R. Anderson, Abco Accessories Ltd

This awkward style with braces and leaders (dots) should not be used:

Chairman: Sir Alfred Adams, O.B.E.

Members: Arbuthnot B. Airey . . . } Ministry of Documents
A. S. Ayling . . . . . . }
Andrew Anton . . . . . . Consultant
A. R. Anderson . . . . . Abco Accessories Ltd

END OF PACKET 1

Separate sheet covering Packet 2

TO PUBLISHER AND PRINTER:
Title: Typing for print
Author: John Westwood
39 Parker Street, London WC2B 5PB

THIS IS PACKET 2 OF TYPESCRIPT
See Inventory below.

22 August 1975

INVENTORY of entire typescript,
of which this packet is part:

Packet 1:
Prelims (folios A to G) and
Chapters 1 to 3 (folios 1 to 36)
Packet 2:
Chapters 4 to 6 (folios 37 to 62)
Packet 3:
Rough sketches for Figs. 1 & 2 and
copy for Tables 1 to 3
(folios 63 to 68)

(Try to contain your whole text within one single packet, so that the publisher's editor can read it as a whole, and with the least possible risk of any parts of it becoming mislaid. Start a second packet, with covering Inventory repeated as above, only when your text is so lengthy that the typescript is more than an inch thick.)

4 Specialized work

4.1 Art, music, drama

When typing articles and books on visual art, give names of works of art underlined for italic: Picasso's *Guernica*, Michelangelo's *David*.

Some art terms are anglicized: atelier, chiaroscuro, cloisonné, collage, décor, faience, fresco (*plural* frescoes), genre, grisaille, motif, repoussé, trecento (1300--1399), quattrocento (1400--1499), campanile. Italicize less common terms: *rilievo*, *trompe l'oeil*, *pinxit*. Other terms: portfolio (*not* shortened to folio), op art, pop art. Type names with care: Brueghel, Caracci, Caravaggio, Cézanne, Claude Lorrain, Cuyp, Degas, Giacometti, Hieronymus Bosch, Michelangelo Buonarroti, Rouault, Ruysdael, Velázquez, Verrocchio.

Major musical works with descriptive titles are usually italicized: *Messiah*, *From the New World*, *Swan Lake*, *Fidelio*, *Aida*, *Götterdämmerung*, *I Pagliacci*, *Tannhäuser*, *Die Walküre*. Definitive titles are given in roman: Chopin's F minor Étude, Gluck's Gavotte in A. Draw accents in.

Unofficial titles, and titles of shorter pieces and songs, are given in roman in quotes: the 'Emperor' Concerto, the 'Eroica' Symphony, 'Heidenröslein', 'Rhapsody in Blue'.

Anglicized terms and names of instruments and organ stops are typed in roman: cor anglais, timpani, vox humana; also terms such as andante, forte, piano, allegretto, repertoire, répétiteur, timbre, embouchure, descant, scherzo: and references such as opus 2 no. 3, *or* op. 2 no. 3. But type with quotes when referring obliquely, e.g. in Wagner's music the 'tremolo' is often used. Italicize *pp*, *ff*, etc.

Type names with care: Dvořák, Grieg (compare British name Greig), Liszt, Rimsky-Korsakov, Saint-Saëns, Shostakovich, Tchaikovsky.

In works of drama, conventions include the use of italic (for stage directions) and square brackets; caps and small caps, marked THUS, may also be used. Italic is also used for songs or verse interpolated between spoken prose passages, and for letters read on stage.

Extracts from copyright works must not be copied without permission: see 1.5.

A

4.2 Science, technology, law

Technical typescripts must be accurate and consistent in spelling, hyphenation, and terminology. Consult specialist dictionaries and standard works; compilers of technical manuals should refer to BS 4884. Make an 'omit points' list (see 2.7, and p. 00). (folio 41)

Underline for italic in zoology and botany for genera, species, varieties: *Daphnia*, *Homo erectus*, *Alnus glutinosa*, but roman for Mammalia, Carnivora, Coniferae. After a common or botanical name, cultivated varieties are in quotes: Cotoneaster 'Cornubia', etc. Type roman lower case for popular names: foxglove, peony, but use italic in lower case for epithets even when derived from personal names: *Berberis darwinii*. In medical work, use italic as required: *thromboangiitis obliterans*, *trachea*.

Capitalize geological strata, periods, regions, and soils: Mesozoic Era, Eocene Period, London Clay.

Type spellings carefully: albumen *and* albumin; arcing; centering (frame for arch) *and* centring; conterminous; co-ordinate with hyphen; gram kilogram and metre (U.S. and U.K. authorities hope soon to agree these spellings for English-language scientific work);

mitring (no e); programme, but program in computing; quasar, radicle, Réaumur, Röntgen etc. The Système International (SI) codifies units and symbols (m for metre, length; s for second, time; V for volt, electric tension; Hz for hertz, frequency; kg for kilogram, mass etc.) as well as capitalization and prefixes for multiplying the units:

Prefix	Symbol	Factor by which the unit is multiplied
tera	T	1 000 000 000 000
giga	G	1 000 000 000
mega	M	1 000 000
kilo	k	1 000
hecto	h	100
deca	da	10
deci	d	0.1
centi	c	0.01
milli	m	0.001
micro	μ (Gk 'mu')	0.000 001
nano	n	0.000 000 001
pico	p	0.000 000 000 001
femto	f	0.000 000 000 000 001
atto	a	0.000 000 000 000 000 001

Thus, a kilometre (km) is a thousand metres (m); a millisecond (ms) is a thousandth of a second (s) etc. Type prefixes in lower case, except T G and M, as in MHz, but all are lower case when spelt out, e.g. megahertz. Use single symbols, e.g. 5.016 km, not 5 km 16 m. Symbols for square and cubic are small superior ^{2} and ^{3}, but m^2 and m^3 can often be typed spelt out as square metres, cubic metres, etc.

The solidus can represent per, so that 40.5 kilograms per metre could be typed as 40.5 kg/m; likewise, rev/min and mile/h are better style than r.p.m. and m.p.h. Thus also: c/s m/s rad/s m/s^2 rad/s^2 kg/m^3 etc. Plurals for technical terms include: apices calculi calices cortices foci genera helices indices laminae maxima minima parhelia radii radices spectra and specula. Type without hyphen where possible, e.g. blood group, foot candle, gamma ray, heat flow, right angle, short circuit, stress rate. But: α-, β-, and γ-rays.

Type certain abbreviated terms and titles without points: ADP LPG BAC CEGB CERN CNAA GNP ICI MRC NASA NPL SI UHF DNA RNA and others.

Abbreviations and symbols are also typed without points: atm b Btu cal cd cgs cm cwt dB dwt dyn ft g gal h hp J kg kWh lb lm m min (minute) ml N nm oz P pdl q rad S sec t W Wh yd; also chemicals Ac Ag Al B C etc. See BS 1991, BS 3763. In text, do not type: a quantity of Ca, but spell out: a quantity of calcium. Type litre in full, as l is easily confused with figure 1. Type km, never Km.

Type with points only where shown: abs. a.c. b.p. calc. cu.m e.m.f. f.p. sq.in (or in^2) cu.in (or in^3) i.r. insol. max. min. (minimum) m.p. mol. ppt. prep. sol. sp.gr. sq.m s.t.p. temp. u.v. vac. vol. wt. and others.

In technical work, type plurals of symbols and SI units without an s: cm cwt dwt ft g in kg lb mm oz yd; type as 7 in or 8 kg, but of course as 7 inches or 8 kilograms with an s if spelt out in full.

A space may be important: m s means metres times seconds, but ms means milliseconds. Note lower case for kelvin, henry, etc.

The decimal point is a full point e.g. 0.5 (British Standard style), or centred, as 0·5. Type and mark large numbers as 1 234 567 (thin #) i.e. requiring the printer to insert thin spaces; commas as in 1,234,567 should not be used in scientific work. Beware when transcribing from the continental style (1,5 per cent and 1.234.567,89) which can confuse the unwary.

In text, do not type a space in four-figure numbers: 7346 km, not 7 (thin #) 436 km. Small decimal quantities require a nought in front thus: 0.12% increase, 0.249 etc. The printer will insert a space, i.e. thin, thick, en, or em (see p. 00 (folio 65)) if marks are inserted thus: a (thin #) b a (thick #) b a (en #) b a (em #) b. Type = and ≠; draw the accent over Å, etc. Mark any ambiguous typewriter characters as necessary: 1 (fig.) l (ell) O (cap O) 0 (nought) 45° (deg) E (set rule not ital.) etc. On some electric machines, mathematical signs can be typed. Or draw neatly in ink such signs as $\sim \equiv \propto > < \geqslant \leqslant \gg \ll \parallel \perp \rightarrow \infty \Sigma \simeq \Pi \surd \pi \Delta \delta \int \oint \nabla \Omega \mu \rightleftharpoons \uparrow \lambda$ and others. Also draw $\times$ and $\div$, because x and ÷ are not clear enough. Type or draw and mark Greek, German, roman or script characters in mathematics as μ (Gk) $\mathfrak{M}$ (Ger) M (rom) $\mathcal{M}$ (scr)

Underline for bold thus, after consulting the publisher, to indicate special technical significance, e.g. (**a**.**b**) for vector quantities. Underline for italic the names of computers and artificial satellites: *Pegasus*, etc.; some publishers mark computer systems in small capitals: ALGOL, etc.

Tell the printer what sort of dash you require, by marking:

Hyphen: *p*-n-butylaniline, *gem*-dichloroethane, L-gluco-peptose, *x*-axis, *E*-layer;

En rule: copper—bismuth alloys (en), time—temperature curves (en), 18--20 seconds (en), Al—Co—Bi alloys (en), stem 30—45 cm high (en);

Minus sign: $(a-b)^2$, $x-y$; (minus)

Em rule or dash: chemical bonds C—H, —O, F—H—; (em)

Two-em rule or long dash: X——B^2 (2 em). (Em, en, etc.: see p. 00.)

Underlining to be printed as such: mark as AB (set rule, not ital), etc.

The above marks resemble those used in normal text (see 2.2) but unspaced technical dashes are (as shown) typed unspaced and marked em.

Bracketing series are [{()}], but [a,b) which is apparently wrong may in fact have mathematical significance.

Printing mathematical and scientific work requires a vast range of special characters. In order to minimize these difficult, slow and expensive complications, you are likely to be <u>asked</u> at the outset to agree to prescribe forms which are easier to set for printing:

$$\underline{n}\text{th} \quad n! \quad (a/b)c \quad (ab)^{-\frac{1}{2}} \quad \surd(a+b) \quad \exp(2\underline{\pi c x}/3\underline{a})$$

rather than:

$$\underline{n}^{th} \quad \lfloor\underline{n} \quad \frac{a}{b}c \quad \frac{1}{\sqrt{ab}} \quad \sqrt{a+b} \quad e^{\frac{2\pi cx}{3\underline{a}}}$$

Very long equations may turn over to the next line in typescript: mark (run on) at the end of the line, as the printer may be able to continue at that point when setting.

Any complicated material should be broken off from the text and started on a fresh line as 'display' or extract style, indented five characters and with extra space above and below. Present it initially in draft form only, taking care to show the correct <u>levels</u> and <u>sizes</u> of letters figures and symbols. Allow ample time for later liaison with the publisher's staff, who may use special marking procedures e.g. with codes for coloured felt pens indicating to the printer the exact details required. BS 1219 Part 3 is not enough by itself. The <u>publisher</u> will decide how to have mathematical work set; (his jargon: photoset e.g. Monophoto, or in hot metal, or impact-set; or artwork to be commissioned, which may be drawn, or with type pulls pasted in, or dry transfer e.g. Letraset, or a mixture of all three).

Where footnotes appear in mathematical work, superior figures are often unsuitable as reference marks, as they might appear to be part of the mathematical expression, and so the traditional footnote marks * † ‡ § || ¶ may have to be drawn in. If the asterisk is already used as a symbol in the text, start with †. Draw these symbols if they cannot be typed; ≠ ǂ and ǂ are not clear enough to represent the dagger or double dagger.

In legal work, use italic for citation of cases, as *Smith* v. *Johnston*, but not for titles of British Acts of Parliament. Acts before 1963 have a comma, e.g. the Finance Act, 1962. The regnal year system of dating as in 10 and 11 Eliz. 2 also ceased after 1962, so that the Finance Act 1963 is numbered as 1963 c. 25. Figures and dates may be spelt out in full. Legal spellings include grantor, judgment, messuage, devest (intransitive verb), etc.

A

4.3 Statistics and tables

Always number tables; apply the methods shown in Tables 1 and 2 where possible. See notes on p. 00 (folio 63). Simple information may often be given in text e.g.: The number of employees has increased; totals for 1970, 1971 and 1972 were 2324, 3010 and 3270 respectively (York 1744, 2410, 2664; Bath 310, 320, 321; and Ely 270, 280, 285). The same facts are more expensive to typeset as a table, even when given (as Table 1) in simple flush-left style without boxes.

Table 1 near here
Copy: see folio 66

If your book has Tables, present your publisher with copy for each Table on a special folio at the end, and not in the text. Reason: Tables must be easily removed from text for separate specialist typesetting. Then, later, they will be put by the printer as near as possible to the places you marked.

Where tables are necessary, type them in flush-left style without boxes, as shown in Tables 1 and 2. This style is readable, easy to type, and easy and economical for the printer to follow. The style throughout each series of tables should be consistent.

In Table 2, the words Registration Figures control four columns, as shown by the width of the typed lines immediately underneath. The subheadings Associates and Licentiates each controls two columns, and the subsubheadings one column. Note also the white space running right across between the 1969 and the 1970 figures, to assist the reader of this large mass of figures.

Table 2 near here →
Copy: see folio 67

Note how four-figure numbers, normally typed without a comma, are shown as 9,374 when they align with groups of five or more figures in the same column.

Break up very large tables into smaller units, or at worst type them on larger paper, with a reference to show correct position in the text, and submit them in a separate packet. It may prove possible to print such tables as double page spreads. In the text, type See Table 9 or See accompanying Table rather than See Table below or following or opposite: it may not be so when printed.

Cash columns should be headed £, or £000, or £ million, with the £ sign aligned left as in Table 2. Italic is sometimes used to indicate the previous year's figures, for comparison. Avoid jargon such as: £5 to £6, upper limit exclusive; £5 to £5.99 is shorter and better. After typing, check all figures with care.

The aim should be to avoid altogether the use of boxes, which are as difficult to type as they are expensive to set up in printers' type; braces {} linking items and leaders (lines of dots) are also to be avoided. See Table 3.

Table 3 near here →
Copy: see folio 68

Copy for tables. If your book is to have statistical or other tables, present the copy for each table on a separate folio at the end, for reasons given above. Then, later, they will be put as near as possible to the places you marked for them (see folios 44 to 46) when the pages are assembled for printing.

A 4.4 Foreign languages

The publisher who is producing a book containing considerable quantities of text in a foreign language may have to employ one of the few printers known to be skilled in setting such work. Each language has its own rules for capitalization, expressing emphasis, and word-breaks at the ends of lines.

Copy should be presented avoiding hyphenation at the ends of lines (see 2.1) if in the form of typescript, or as very neat handwriting, or as a photocopy of a printed or typed original. For notes on typographical detail for some European languages, see study lists 6.3, 6.4, and also Hart.

Usage as regards quotation marks in continental languages is quite different from English. In fiction, they are often omitted in dialogue, but each new paragraph starts with a dash. In Spanish text, questions are shown thus: ¿Quien sabe?

You as author or amanuensis must undertake proof correction, or if necessary pass it to another expert skilled in the typographical usage of the foreign language.

Camera-ready copy (see 5.4) may perhaps be produced on an electric typewriter with foreign characters, using a one-time carbon ribbon, but only after full co-operation with the publisher to determine the width of line, etc.

A short extract in a rare foreign language which is already in printed form may be treated as an illustration original for reproduction: see 5.1. First submit a photocopy indicating which way up, any lines to be omitted, etc. The publisher will then arrange to have the original (not the photocopy) properly photographed so as to be suitable for printing.

O

A 4.5 Fiction

In narrative text, reading should not be impeded by unnecessary bold type, capitalization or italicization of odd words, over-punctuation, or other features creating a visually patchy effect. Numbers may often be typed spelt out: see 2.9. Accents proper to foreign words should be carefully drawn in, but roman rather than italic may be used for partially anglicized words: see study list 6.3.

A 4.6 The author and the editor

When you are commissioned to write an article, chapter, or book for an established series, follow the series style as regards the heading system, spellings, especially of proper names, and punctuation -- nevertheless, the editor may alter details later.

Newspapers and magazines have their own special customs as regards typed copy. Paper may be smaller than A4; but allow very wide margins. Leave three blank lines between paragraphs. Paragraphs must always end on the same folio, and not continue on the next.

Many journalists would type 'The prime minister said . . .' where in a book it would read 'The Prime Minister said . . .' The aim is avoidance of pomposity. Use an active construction rather than passive. Omit useless prepositions: check up, check out, test out, end up. In some newspapers, foreign words may appear without accents: debacle, denouement; if accents cannot be printed you cannot use words like pâté and résumé. Simplifying Khrushchev to Kruschev and the like may be allowable: do not degrade the correct foreign pronunciation too far. Re-phrase 'in this country' or 'our legal system' if your work is likely to be read in U.S.A. or elsewhere. Your editor may ban cliché-words, e.g. amazing, astounding, and/or, auspices, best of health, cannot help but, crash programme, consensus of opinion, debut, definitely, demise, en masse, en route, excessively, fatality, finalize, glamour, hail from, hectic, inter alia, initiate, interesting to note, pay tribute to, prior to, quite, reside, sensational, shambles, terminate, terrific, tremendous, via, very, vicinity of, viz., wend one's way, yuletide, Xmas.

Compile an 'omit points' list (see 2.7). Some editors[1] omit points in UK USA USSR TUC VAT EEC AD BC and other abbreviations.

For copy which is to be printed as part of a series, authors may mark the headings as follows. First, write (NOT FOR COPY) on the outside of two or three pages already printed in the series style, and on these pages mark the printed headings [A], [B], [C] etc. to indicate the grades of importance. Then mark the typescript headings with similar letters, to show correlation; write on the cover of the typescript (SEE STYLE SPECIMEN HEREWITH).

---

1 Note to editors and designers. Decorations and degrees (see p. 00 (folio 20)) may be marked up for caps or small caps, with or without full points. Typescripts which are in the style shown at 2.2 may be given a covering note, thus:

NOTE TO PRINTER. Hyphens typed thus, hi-fi, in copy: SET AS HYPHEN.
Spans thus in copy, 1914--18: SET AS UNSPACED EN RULE.
Dashes (pauses) thus -- in copy: SET AS UNSPACED EM RULE.*
Long dashes thus --- in copy: SET AS 2-EM RULE.*

*Or specify here spaced en or em rule. Style of author's copy would not be affected. Methods shown would work with OCR.

A 4.7 List structures and charts

Complicated technical sequences, legislation, and logical patterns may sometimes be explained either by list structures or by charts. A simple example follows. First, a list structure (in turnover indent style) which is easy both for typing and for the printer:

1. Turn on ignition. Does red light come on?

   If yes, go to question 2. If no, go to question 3.

2. Start engine. Does it fire readily?

   If yes, you are ready to move. If no, go to question 4.

3. Is battery properly connected?

   If no, connect. Then go back to question 1. If yes, etc.

4. Is the fuel gauge reading above zero? etc.

A diagrammatic chart (see Fig. 1) may be a more attractive method of presentation, but this would require special artwork and reproduction arrangements which might delay production and increase cost.

Figure 1 near here
Rough sketch:
see folio 64

(Figure 1 would properly appear at this point in the text. When your book is printed, the publisher would put such a figure as near as he can to the indicated point.)

List structures will be the better method for some themes, while for others a chart or diagram will be preferable. Much depends on the kind of reader for whom you are writing.

Your publisher may prefer list structures. This is because he may wish to omit illustrations altogether, for economic reasons. Try to plan your typescript initially on this basis.

5 Illustrations

5.1 Presentation

Illustrations can be attractive, and diagrams can explain ideas better than text. But all printing is cheaper and quicker to produce without them. (Never, never paste illustrations into your typescript.)

Colour is particularly expensive. If, after consultation, your publisher agrees to illustrations, you should mark approximate positions in typescript margins, as on p. 00, and provide only rough pencil sketches on separate folios in a separate packet: see p. 00.

This treatment will suffice to indicate any kind of diagram or illustration, including those which you may already have in a finished state. Below each sketch, you may add encircled notes to the publisher to state owner of copyright, if any, and any permissions obtained. You will also say if you have the finished illustration already available. Await advice from the publisher before making any further arrangements with an artist or photographer.

Your rough pencil sketches will give an impression of the intended effect (see p. 00). Number the line diagrams as Fig. 1, 2 etc., and tone illustrations as Plate I, II etc. (The system may for technical reasons be subject to later change by the publisher, but do not worry about this. You cannot plan for it.) In your typescript margin, for each illustration, write e.g. (Fig. 1 near here). The position can only be approximate; the ideal position in the text cannot always be achieved exactly when the printed pages are made up.

Where you can, group small line diagrams together so as to make up full pages, rather than scatter them between paragraphs of text. Technical diagrams sometimes have a scale: this must be in drawn linear form, not numerical as 1:10, because the latter kind of scale is falsified if the drawing is printed in a reduced size. Give both metric and imperial dimensions.

There are various distinct categories of illustration; see p. 00. (folio 64)
Include also copy for captions on suitably headed folios (see 5.3).

Your publisher will arrange the necessary preparation of high quality artwork, i.e. finished drawings and photographs. If you are contributing some yourself, number each item e.g. (Fig. 1) or (Plate I) very lightly with a B pencil on the back, or (better) on a flap. Check accuracy of numbering: the same numbers may actually appear in text references, or list of illustrations, or index references. Number any colour transparencies on their enclosing envelopes.

Your publisher will certainly wish to advise you on the subject before expenditure is undertaken; unsuitable material includes photographs which are matt-finished, anaemic in tone, creased, marked, dented, heavily rubber-stamped on the back, or damaged by inadequate packing in transit. Captions should not be stuck on the backs.

When the publisher calls for your own items -- and not before -- present them unmounted, in a packet, and enclosing a list of the items, to avoid confusion or loss. When packing, never use paper-clips: they cause dents which show up as marks in the printed reproduction. Pack the items flat (not rolled) between thick cardboard, with care; they are valuable. Deliver your artwork items personally if they are too large for the post, or if they are irreplaceable, or late.

A 5.2 Lettering on illustrations

Any necessary lettering to appear on diagrams or maps will need to be in style with the text as regards spelling and capitalization. As the publisher may decide to arrange for specialized techniques for inserting high-quality lettering, your copy for such lettering should be typed out in columns and suitably headed, on separate numbered folios in the final packet. It is thus ready for typesetting.

Where possible, move any large quantity of such lettering from the diagram itself to the caption under the illustration. It is easier to print there, and leaves the illustration less cluttered.

A 5.3 Captions, acknowledgements

Number the copy for each caption as for the figure or plate it belongs to. Do not attach copy for captions to the illustrations in any way, but present it separate from the text, listed in double-spaced typing, suitably headed.

Footnotes to captions would be a cumbersome nuisance, and should be avoided. Pack late afterthoughts at proof stage into available spaces at the ends of paragraphs. But only if they are absolutely essential; the aim should be minimum alterations on proofs.

Do not reproduce copyright illustration material without permission; your publisher will advise.

Give acknowledgements in a special section in the prelims, or under the actual illustration or table, or in the list of illustrations, or in two such places.

O

A 5.4 Camera-ready copy

For small editions of specialized books, electric typewriters with carbon ribbon and variable spacing may be used by publishers to make quite presentable originals of the whole book ready for direct reproduction. Such typewriter keyboarding by specialists is called strike-on or impact-set composition.

Close co-operation between author, editor, designer and typist is required in order to achieve good overall results. In many cases only one or two sizes of typing face will be available. Headings will therefore be planned to exploit effects of inter-line spacing and indenting. Underlining would tend to look amateurish in the final product: avoid it if possible.

Copy will be prepared on high-quality white paper, and will be made up into pages by specialists with illustrations pasted in at the proper points. The whole is then photographed and reproduced lithographically. Similar methods may be used for the production of artwork for complicated diagrams, perhaps combined with drawing and dry-transfer work.

6 Study lists

6.1 Proper names and titles

The study lists which follow are intended for typists who wish to be certain of the proper names and foreign words liable to occur in authors' drafts. Common words in a foreign language may gradually acquire different spelling when they are borrowed for use in English; but proper names, having owners, are looked after more carefully.

Unanglicized foreign names prefixed with de or d' are styled with lower case, as de Gaulle, d'Annunzio, d'Arsonval. When anglicized, they may take a capital: De Quincey, De L'Isle, D'Amato. If in doubt, follow the style of the owner's signature. Likewise van and von: Van Gogh.

List of proper names and titles: Thomas à Becket; Abélard and Heloïse; capital A for Aborigines in Australia; Anouilh; Apennines, but Appalachians; Athenaeum Club; Averroës; Baghdad (but U.S. style Bagdad); Basle; Berkhamsted, but Hemel Hempstead and Hampstead; Bournemouth but Bournville; Britannia and Britannic, but Brittany; Brussels; Cape Town; D'Oyly Carte; Anton Chekhov; Chou en-Lai; Richard Cœur de Lion; Colosseum (Rome) but Coliseum (London); Colquhoun; Crécy; Cymru, Cymry; Dáil Éireann; Éamon de Valera; Domesday Book; Edgbaston, Edgware; Eōthen; Ex-President; Edward FitzGerald; Frankfurt am Main, am Oder; Fräulein (abbr. Frl.); Führer; Fujiyama; Gandhi; Garter King-of-Arms; Gautama Buddha; Genghis Khan; Ghent; Gollancz; Gray's Inn; Guildford, but Guilford Street, London; Gutenberg; Habsburg; Hong Kong; Houyhnhnm; Ben Jonson; Jakob Jordaens; Juggernaut; Thomas à Kempis; Khartoum; Omar Khayyám; Kingston upon Hull, upon Thames; Lao-tsze; Lapland, but a Lapp; Larousse; La Tène; D. H. Lawrence, T. E. Lawrence; St Lawrence (Canada); W. Le Queux;

Lhasa; Liège; Linnean Society; Ljubljana; Llanelli; Luxembourg Palace in Paris, but Luxemburg; MacDonald, Macdonald, McDonald, M^c^Donald, M‘Donald with turned comma: all treated in alphabetical lists as Mac; Flora MacDonald; Niccolò Machiavelli; Magdalen College Oxford but Magdalene College Cambridge; Muhammad; Manichaean; Mercedes (German car) but Mercédès (French name); le Métro, Paris; Middlesbrough; Monte Cristo; Morocco; Mycenaean; Nebuchadnezzar (also other Bible versions); Newcastle upon Tyne, under Lyme; Nibelungenlied; Nietzsche; Nijmegen; Nuremberg (exception to rule 'burg means town, berg means mountain'); Oistrakh; Pantheon, Rome, but Panthéon, Paris; Sir Perceval; Plynlimon; Procurator-fiscal; Pwllheli; Qatar; Rolls-Royce; Romania; Romanov dynasty; Romansh; Earl of Rosebery; Roussillon; The Rubáiyát; Runnymede; 's Gravenhage; St James's Square, etc., in London; Sakyamuni; Sa Majesté (masc. and fem.); Samarkand; Sanskrit; Santa Fé, S. America; São Paolo; Savile Row; Scafell Pikes but Sca Fell; Scheherazade; Schleswig-Holstein; Schwarzwald; Schweitzer; Schwyz (canton); a Sergeant, but Serjeant in Army lists, and in Law; Seven Years War; Sèvres; Shakespeare; Jack Sheppard; Solzhenitsyn; Edmund Spenser; Sri Lanka; Srinagar; Mme de Staël; George and Robert Stephenson, but R. L. Stevenson; Robert Stevenson (lighthouses); Laurence Sterne; Struwwelpeter; House of Stuart; Sub-Lieutenant; the Sûreté, Paris; Surgeon-General; Taoism; Tarbert and Tarbet, Scotland; Tatar or Tartar; Tauchnitz; Teesside; Tenerife; Tolstoy; Tonbridge, but Tunbridge Wells; Tsar, Tsarevich, Tsarina; Tyrol; Uffizi; Uppsala; Valladolid; Vergilius or Virgil, 70--19 B.C., but also Vergil, A.D. 1470--1555; Very pistol; Vice-President of the United States; Wedgwood; Weihaiwei; Welch Fusiliers but Welsh Guards; Westmorland; Wigton and Wigtown; Württemberg; Zaïre; Zeeland and Zealand; Zurich.

Some of the foregoing are in fact shown in anglicized form: the Germans spell Nuremberg as Nürnberg. Similarly, the Yugoslavs spell Yugoslavia as Jugoslavija; other 'foreign' spellings, which need to be recognized even if not used, include Deutschland, España, Österreich, and Schweiz, Suisse, or Svizzera. The initials CCCP are really the Cyrillic letters for SSSR. In Dutch, ij is treated as a compound letter, so that place-names include such forms as IJsselsteijn. Munich is München to the Germans, but Monaco di Baviera to the Italians. (Rees gives further examples.)

Foreign titles and degrees include such oddities as B. ès L., B. ès S.; Mme Mlle and Ste are typed without a full point.

Some British family titles differ from similar place-names: Ailesbury, Aylesbury; Carnarvon, Caernarvon; Scarbrough, Scarborough; Zetland, Shetland. Plurals in proper names: note 'the three Marys', <u>not</u> Maries; Mr and Mrs Perry are 'the Perrys'.

6.2 Anglicized words

Foreign words are welcome in English, when they convey a shade of meaning which no English word conveys: bizarre, debonair, gauche. Naturalized words are typed without underlining.

The study list includes some words which tend to be over-used by some writers: adieu (plural adieux), aide-de-camp, al fresco, alias, alleluia (biblical hallelujah), apache, apartheid, apéritif, aplomb, apropos of, argot, attaché, au pair (girl), aurora borealis, autobahn, baksheesh, beau idéal, belles-lettres, bizarre, blasé, blitz, bloc, blond (fem. blonde), bona fide, bona fides, bon vivant, not the same as bon viveur; bourgeois, braggadocio, bric-à-brac, café, canyon, chaise-longue, chaperon, chargé d'affaires, chateau; cicada, compare cigala; ci-devant, claque, cliché, clientele, communiqué, concierge, confrère, connoisseur, contretemps, conversazione, cortège, crèche, crêpe, cul-de-sac, débâcle; debonair, debris (no accent); début; débutant, fem. débutante; décor, delicatessen, dénouement; depot, detour (no accent), dilettante, doctrinaire, doyen, echelon, éclat, élite, embonpoint, embouchement, ennui, ensemble, entourage, entrée, entrepreneur, ersatz, espionage, espresso coffee, extempore, façade, facetiae; facia over shop but fascia under cornice in architecture; farouche; fête, fêted; fiancé, fiancée; fjord or fiord; flair, flambeau, flamenco, fleur-de-lis, foyer; fra (brother, friar), fracas; furore; gamin, gamine; gasconade; gâteau; gauche, gaucherie; gendarme, genre, giaour, glacier, graffito, gratis, guerrilla, habeas corpus, hauteur, hegira, hubris, impasse, incommunicado, kaput, kepi, kudos, lakh, legionnaire, leitmotiv, lèse-majesté, levee, liaison, liqueur, literati, loggia, maladroit, marionette, matinée, mêlée, menu, migraine, milieu, minutiae, misalliance, morale, mynheer, naïve, narghile, négligé, nom de plume, nuance, obit, ohone, onus, ormolu, oubliette, padre (colloq., chaplain), palliasse, papier mâché, parole, parvenu, patois, peccadillo, penchant, persiflage, piazza, pince-nez; piqué, fabric, and piquet, card game; placebo, plafond, podestà, poste restante, potpourri, précis, première, prie-dieu, prima facie, pronto; protégé, protégée; provenance, putsch, quid pro quo, quondam, quorum, raconteur, Realpolitik, recherché, reconnaissance, regime or régime, rendezvous, requiem, résumé, reveille, au revoir!, rigor mortis, riposte, role, roué, salaam, sang-froid, sans serif, sari, savant, schnapps, seance, seriatim, serviette, sheikh, soi-disant; soigné, fem. soignée; soirée, sola topi, souchong, soupçon, sputnik, stiletto, subpoena, suede, sufi, suttee, terra firma, terra incognita, tête-à-tête, toupee, tovarich, vade-mecum, valkyrie, vendetta, verbatim, versus, via, vice versa, virtuoso, visa, viva voce, volte-face, wadi; wagon-lit, wagons-lits; yashmak.

Accents have been omitted from some of the above: château has become chateau. Type exactly as in the above list, when treating as anglicized. It is easy to use a foreign word in the wrong way; for example, the term nom de plume is never used in France: it is of purely English manufacture.

A 6.3 Foreign words in roman or italic

Do not over-use foreign words. If they are necessary, some may (in addition to list 6.2) be typed without underlining for italic, particularly in works of fiction, or popular periodicals, or newspapers: ad infinitum, ad nauseam, agent provocateur, allons!, amour propre, ancien régime, appliqué, après moi, arrondissement, auberge, au contraire, au fait, au fond, auf wiedersehen, au naturel, au revoir, auto-da-fé, à votre santé!, bête noire, Bierkeller, billet doux, bonhomie, bureau de change, canaille, carte blanche, cause célèbre, c'est la guerre, chef d'œuvre, chère amie, chéri, ciao, circa, congé, coup d'état, curriculum vitae, danke schön, démarche, de rigueur, de trop, élan; émigré, émigrée, en bloc, en avant, en fête, en masse, en route, esprit de corps, ex officio, fait accompli, faux pas, fiacre, fiesta, fin de siècle, garçon, habitué, haute couture, hors de combat, in camera, in flagrante delicto, in situ, inter alia, in toto, je ne sais quoi, lacuna, laissez-faire, laissez-passer, lorgnette, ma foi!, malaise, mal de mer, mañana, marchese, mardi gras, matelot, mea culpa, ménage, merci, métier, mise en scène, modus operandi, monde, multum in parvo, naïveté, n'est-ce pas?, noblesse oblige, nom de guerre, oui, outré, panache, par excellence, pavé, per capita, per se, petit déjeuner, pièce de résistance, pied-à-terre, plat du jour, Polizei, pourboire, prima donna, pro rata, purée, raison d'être, rapport, rapprochement, régime, Reichstag, risqué; salon, sauve qui peut, savoir-faire, señor (Span.), senhor (Portug.), Signor (Ital.); siècle, s'il vous plaît, sotto voce, status quo, sub judice, svelte, tour de force, tout court, valet de chambre, verboten, vis-à-vis.

Accents and spelling should in all cases be copied with care, as the words in this list are not regarded as naturalized to the extent that liberties may be taken with the correct foreign form.

The words in the above list, being not fully anglicized, would look a little strange in serious works if they were printed in roman. Therefore, in such work, type them underlined for italic: <u>ad infinitum</u>, <u>ad nauseam</u>, <u>agent provocateur</u>, <u>allons</u>! etc. . . . <u>tour de force</u>, <u>tout court</u>, <u>valet de chambre</u>, <u>verboten</u>, <u>vis-à-vis</u>.

A specialized and confused area is that of catering and cookery, where many words of foreign origin, mostly French, are employed. In borrowing either way, errors of spelling sometimes take root, e.g. bifteck, bistecca. Careful typing of foreign spelling and accents makes proper pronunciation possible. Refer to Collins or to reputable works on cookery published by Faber or Penguin.

Text for cookery books and the like will be unnecessarily confusing if some foreign terms are in italic and others not; therefore in such books and in menus all may be in roman. Some notable proper names have traps of spelling, such as Veuve Clicquot, Kümmel, Daiquiri, Madeira, Riesling, Mâcon, Roquefort, and Gruyère.

Anglicized words which should not be capitalized or italicized include: à la carte, barbecue, caviare, chartreuse, consommé, curaçao, éclair, entrée, frangipane, frankfurter, fricandeau, fricassee, gateau, hors d'œuvre, olla podrida, omelet, pilaff, pilau, ragout, smorgasbord, spaghetti, table d'hôte, vol-au-vent, wienerschnitzel, yogurt *or* yoghourt, etc. The accents and spellings, if slightly different from the original form, are acceptable as shown.

In occasional text references in books not primarily concerned with the subject of food, terms not yet anglicized should be typed underlined for italic: *à la française*, *à la provençale*, *assiettes*, *au gratin*, *béarnaise*, *bifteck* (beefsteak), *bœuf*, *café*, *chou-fleur*, *choux de Bruxelles*, *compote*, *crèmes*, *crêpe*, *entrées*, *entremets*, *fondue*, *frit* (*frite*, *frites*), *fromages*, *gelées*; *glace* (ice) but *glacé* (glazed); *huîtres*, *légumes*, *œufs*; *pâte* (paste) but *pâté* (pie): English pâté is a liver paste; *pâtisserie*, *pêche*, *plat du jour*; *poissons*, *potages*, *ragoût*, *relevés*, *rôtis*, *Sauerkraut*, *sauté*, *suprême*, *truite*, *veau*, etc.

A

6.4 Foreign words in italic

Underline for setting in italic all foreign words not shown in lists 6.1 to 6.3, e.g. the following: à bas, ab initio, addio, à deux, ad hoc, adresse, à droite, ad valorem, affaire de coeur, affaire d'honneur, à gauche, aîné, allez-vous-en!, amende honorable, anglice, Angst; août and other months in French; à outrance, à pied, a posteriori, appui, après-midi, a priori, au grand sérieux; autres temps, autres moeurs; ben venuto, bidonville, bon goût, bon mot, caffè, c'est à dire, ci-gît, clin d'oeil, cocotte; comme ci, comme ça; coup de grâce, coup d'oeil, crime passionel, da, de règle, demi-monde, double entendre, en clair, enosis, en règle, esprit, étude, flèche (arrow), frère, Gastarbeiter (plural same), grazie, hoch!, hvala, idée fixe, imprimatur, inconnu (fem. inconnue), ingénue, in hac parte, insh'allah, ja, jeu d'esprit, lapsus linguae, lettre de cachet, maître, mauvaise honte, moeurs, mores; mur (wall) but mûr (ripe); né (fem. née), nein, ne plus ultra, niet, non, nota bene, obiit, objet d'art, oeil, oeuvres, opus, pace, padre (father, priest, not chaplain), par avion, par hasard, pari passu, peccavi; pêche means peach or fishing, but péché means sin; pension, Père (of priest), persona non grata; peut-être, pinxit, pis aller, più, placet, politesse, poseur, primeur, procès-verbal, puîné, pur sang, qua, quien sabe?, quipu; rédacteur (French), Redakteur (German); règle, Reichskanzler, rez-de-chaussée, sake; French sale means dirty but salé means salted; Schadenfreude, si, soeur de charité, son et lumière, succès de scandale, sui generis, tabula rasa, tant mieux, tant pis, timbre-poste, touché!, tutoyer, ultra vires, vale!; vieille, compare vielle, veille; Wanderjahre, Wehrmacht, Weltschmerz. (All German nouns are capitalized.)

END OF PACKET 2

Separate sheet covering Packet 3

TO PUBLISHER AND PRINTER: Title: Typing for print Author: John Westwood 39 Parker Street, London WC2B 5PB

THIS IS PACKET 3 See Inventory below.

22 August 1975 INVENTORY of entire typescript, of which this packet is part: Packet 1: Prelims (folios A to G) and Chapters 1 to 3 (folios 1 to 36) Packet 2: Chapters 4 to 6 (folios 37 to 62) Packet 3: Rough sketches for Figs. 1 & 2 and copy for Tables 1 to 3 (folios 63 to 68)

Final note on illustrations and tables. All the packets of your typescript should if possible be sent together in one parcel to the publisher. If your book is to have illustrations or tables, the final packet of copy should comprise rough sketches for the illustrations or copy for the tables, all on a filing tag (see folio 65). Even if they are crucial to the chain of thought in your book, the publisher will prefer them as a separate packet. The publisher's editor will be able to refer across from the text to the illustration packet easily enough, when he is assessing your work.

The reason for requiring the separate packet is that illustrations and tables must be capable of easy removal en bloc, so that the públisher's staff can make the necessary arrangements for obtaining drawings, page layouts, photographs, printing blocks, and specialist typesetting for tables, captions, etc. All this is done quite apart from typesetting the text. Then, later, the illustrations and tables will be put as near as possible to the places you marked for them, when the pages are finally assembled for printing.

Rough sketch for Fig. 1 (see folio 50)

Each rough sketch should be on a separate folio

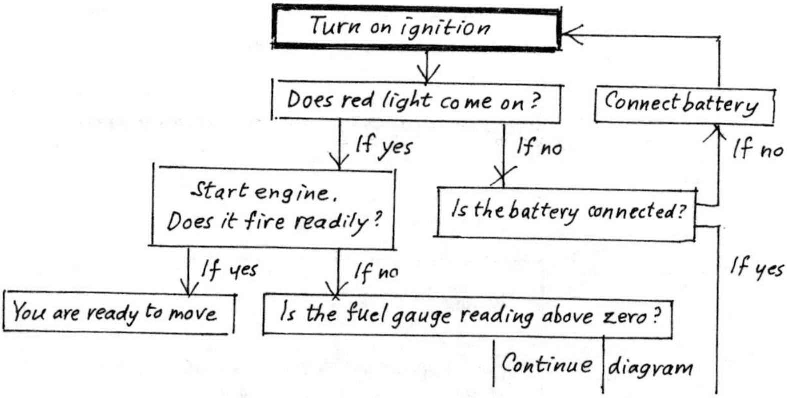

Line drawings are in black ink, without grey tones. A specialist artwork studio may, on the publisher's instructions, make the actual final drawing: a diagram, a graph, a flow chart, a map or plan, a creative imaginative illustration, an orthographic drawing, an isometric drawing, or a perspective drawing or 'exploded' view of a technical subject; or (p. 00) folio 65 reproduced type specimens etc.

Halftone illustrations should -- despite the name -- be in a full range of tone from black through grey to white. Halftones are based on photographs or wash drawings, and require to be printed on the right kind of paper to be effective.

Colour originals may be in line or tone, and may be in the form of drawings or transparencies. Line is cheaper to print than tone.

Rough sketch for Fig. 2 (to appear at or near end of book)

Typography

Technical authors may need to study the technology of printers' typefaces. Other authors and typists are unlikely to need more than is given here.

1 Type HYPHENS thus: hi-fi; they will be printed thus: hi-fi. See 2.2

Type SPANS thus: 1914--18, or the London--Dover road: they will be printed as 1914–18, London–Dover road, using what the printer calls an en rule (an en is the width of a half-square of type, thus ▯).

Type DASHES (pauses) as spaced double hyphens -- as here -- but they *may* be printed—as here—using what the printer calls an em rule (an em: width of square of type □) or – as here – using spaced en rules.

Type LONG DASHES thus ---; they may be printed thus —— using what the printer calls a 2-em rule.

2 Punch a hole through the top left-hand corner of each folio. Assemble folios in loose packets by threading on a filing tag.

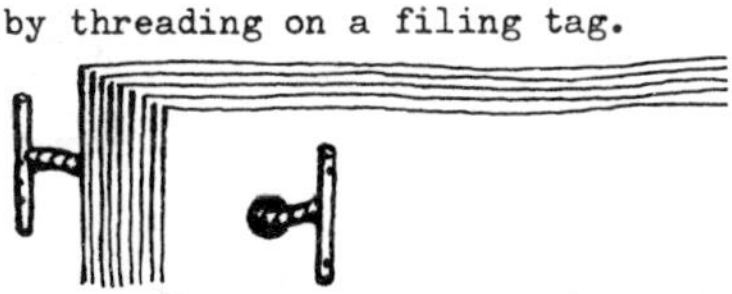

This method permits the printer to share out the typescript to several compositors, so that all can begin typesetting simultaneously. This cannot be done if the typescript has been bound.

3 For each typeface, the printer usually has CAPS, lower case, *ITALIC CAPS*, *italic lower case*, **BOLD CAPS, bold lower case,** and sometimes SMALL CAPS.

4 For printing your text, the publisher's staff will select from the printer's range of typefaces, among which may be:

Baskerville Times
Bembo Univers medium

5 The above four specimens are in 10-point size (72 pts = 1 inch).

This is Baskerville 6pt
This is Baskerville 8pt
This is Baskerville 12pt

If 1 extra point of white is added between lines of 10 pt, it would be called 10 on 11 body (10/11 pt).

6 Above are Monotype faces. There are also other systems:

Monophoto: Baskerville
Linotype slugset: Baskerville
IBM Press Roman for litho
IBM Univers for litho

7 Lining figures ALIGN CAPS: 1267.
Italic lining figs.: 126790 ALIGN.
Old Style figs. align with lower case and small caps: 126790 abc A.D. 1970.

Either lining or old style figs. will be used throughout your book.

8 Spaces, mathematics and science:
(ab) unspaced. See folio 42.
(a b) with thin space
(a b) with thick space
(a b) with en space
(a   b) with em space

SPECIAL NOTE TO EDITORS, DESIGNERS, AND PRINTERS: The footnote on folio 49 refers to marking up copy.
BS 5261 Part 1 is recommended as a general study of copy preparation.

Some details have been made up with special printer's type proofs, to illustrate points clearly. They are printed true size as stated.

O

(66)

Copy for Table 1

(see text folio 44)

Table 1: Number of employees

	York	Bath	Ely	Total
1970	1744	310	270	2324
1971	2410	320	280	3010
1972	2664	321	285	3270

Note: copy for each of these Tables should be arranged in the centre of a separate numbered folio of full A4 size

(67)

Copy for Table 2

(see text folio 45)

Table 2. [Style for complex tables.] Registration figures and income

	Registration figures				Income		
	Associates		Licentiates		Registration		Club
Year	Bankers Order	Annual Subscr	Bankers Order	Annual Subscr	Bkrs Os £	Subscr £	£
1965	4728	4821	3291	4010	47,203	60,273	9,374
1966	4870	4976	3423	4651	48,301	65,334	10,987
1967	4960	5008	3221	4559	49,863	66,307	13,305
1968	5012	4998	3561	4778	50,956	67,395	15,888
1969	5210	5660	3331	4353	52,886	69,123	20,853
1970	5371	5544	3098	4326	53,443	69,448	26,841
1971	5299	4553	3688	4441	52,555	70,431	28,853
1972	5001	5443	3388	4387	54,674	67,375	29,762
1973	4720	5377	3258	4567	56,775	71,666	30,121
1974	5023	5099	3421	4678	56,777	70,342	30,541

PRINTER: SET THIN SPACES INSTEAD OF COMMAS

(68)

Copy for Table 3

(see text folio 46)

Table 3. [How not to present a table: awkward boxes, including two sideways; typing is difficult to centre in boxes.] Membership figures and income

		No. of Regional Offices	No. of Local Branches	Included in totals on right		Totals of regd members	Annual total income £
				Members paying to Regl Offices	Members paying by Bkrs Orders		
1970	Estimated memb'ship	6	18	701	783	2374	23,840
1971	figures	7	20	836	904	3010	31,277
1972	....	7	21	870	950	3270	33,149

END OF PACKET 3: END OF BOOK